For the *Love* of *Cats*

Purrfect Felines

Dena Harris

Publications International, Ltd.

Dena Harris is a popular cat humorist and freelance writer published in *Chicken Soup for the Cat Lover's Soul, Cats & Kittens, I Love Cats,* and more. She is also the author of *Lessons in Stalking...Adjusting to Life With Cats.* Dena, her husband, and their two formerly stray cats live in rural North Carolina, where Dena is constantly trying to figure out how to bring a third cat into the home without her husband's knowledge.

ACKNOWLEDGMENTS

Page 31: The card is a copy of a photograph taken in 1996 by Kylie Bishop for the State Library of New South Wales of the statue by John Cornwall at the State Library of New South Wales, Sydney.

Pages 182–183: "The Naming of the Cats" from OLD POSSUM'S BOOK OF PRACTICAL CATS, © 1939 by T.S. Eliot and renewed 1967 by Esme Valerie Eliot, reprinted by permission of Harcourt, Inc.

We'd also like to thank the following people for their contributions:

Amy D. Shojai and Irene Gizzi; Glenda Moore for "How to Give a Cat a Pill"; Stuart Hample for "Happy Cat Day"; Wendy Liebman; and Liz Palika

Louis Weber, CEO
Publications International, Ltd.
7373 North Cicero Avenue
Lincolnwood, Illinois 60712

Permission is never granted for commercial purposes.

ISBN-13: 978-1-4127-1277-4

ISBN-10: 1-4127-1277-7

Manufactured in China.

8 7 6 5 4 3 2 1

Library of Congress Control Number: 2006900100

Contents

Chapter One

Feline Mystique
Cats Through the Ages

"*What sort of philosophers are we, who know absolutely nothing of the origin and destiny of cats?*"
—Henry David Thoreau

CATS IN HISTORY

OUR RELATIONSHIP WITH CATS dates back almost 4,000 years. Over time, cats have traded a presence in the wild for a sheltered, more comfortable existence cradled in the lap of their owners. We have been the better for it ever since.

Humans have never quite known what to make of our domesticated—yet independent (some would say "untamed")—feline friends. The ancient Egyptians solved the riddle by associating cats with gods, worshiping them, dedicating temples to them, and carving cat statues. Killing a cat was a crime punishable by death. Ancient Egyptians staged elaborate mourning ceremonies at the death of a cat, and the mummified remains of hundreds of thousands of cats have since been discovered.

Other societies used the cat as a symbol of liberty; the feline streak of independence was a natural match for the political ideal of freedom. Cats have since been celebrated as seers, talismans, and the forbearers of both good and ill luck.

In the thirteenth century, cats met a harsh fate at the hands of the church, which declared the feline to be in league with witches and the devil.

Today, no longer a devil or a god, the cat has taken her rightful place as a beloved companion. Her observant stare and constant purr are a gentle acknowledgment that through the ages, she has always kept her own counsel—and endured.

"Thousands of years ago, cats were worshiped as gods. Cats have never forgotten this."

—ANONYMOUS

*A*CCORDING TO FOLKLORE, Noah feared having lions on the ark. God answered Noah's prayer and caused the great cats to fall asleep. Soon Noah realized that the mouse was also a danger. Again Noah prayed for help; this time God caused the sleeping lion to sneeze, and out sprang the world's first cat.

*"T*he cat was created when the lion sneezed."
—ARABIAN PROVERB

The Madonna's Tribute to the Tabby Cat

*B*ABY JESUS WAS unable to sleep. His mother beseeched the stable animals for assistance, but none could help. Then a small, shy tabby cat stepped forward. After first thoroughly cleaning herself (so as not to offend the mother or her child), the striped gray kitten snuggled beside baby Jesus. Her rich purr filled the stable with a cat lullaby, and the baby fell asleep with a smile. The Madonna touched the kitten on her forehead in grateful benediction. From that day forward, all proper tabby cats wore an *M* on their brow in honor of the service they performed for the Madonna.

CATS IN EARLY RELIGIONS

- Jaguars and eagles were the symbols of the two orders of the Aztec warrior knights. The warriors believed wearing the skin of a jaguar gave them extraordinary powers.

- During the sixth century B.C., the Chavín civilization of Peru worshiped a cougar god.

- The Zapotecs of ancient Mexico honored a jaguar god called Cosijo.

- Birman cats guarded the Buddhist temple of Lao-Tsun.

- Siamese cats were the cherished companions of royalty in ancient Siam.

- Early Christianity welcomed the cat as a symbol of motherhood.

Stone carving of Cosijo

Cats and Miacids

WHAT'S A MIACID? The miacid is the great-great-granddaddy of all cats. The weasellike creatures with meat-shearing teeth first appeared 61 million years ago and lived in forests. Their retractable claws and agile bodies made them equally at home hunting on the ground or scrambling through the trees. Due to their larger brains, the miacids became expert hunters and outlived other carnivorous mammals.

Miacid

© Pat Ortega 1995

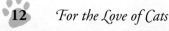

Saber-tooth cat

Miacids eventually evolved into a variety of carnivores, including the civet cat, one of the first members of the cat family. Other evolutions include the *Pseudaelurus*, an ancestor of domestic and great cats. *Smilodon*, a type of saber-tooth cat, evolved from *Pseudaelurus* and first appeared approximately one million years ago. These cats became extinct about 11,000 years ago when the animals they preyed on died out.

*I*N OR OUT? It is said the Manx lost her tail
when Noah shut the door to the ark too
soon and cut it off.

For the Love of Cats

"How we behave toward cats here below determines our status in heaven."

—Robert A. Heinlein

How Cats Came to Be

The Sun and Moon held a contest to see who could create the finest animal. Sun fashioned a lion and greatly impressed the other gods. Moon was filled with jealousy and created a sprightly cat. But the gods mocked Moon's imitation lion. Sun created a mouse as a sign of his contempt. Moon desperately tried again and created a monkey, but the monkey received even greater derision. Furious over her humiliation, Moon caused eternal strife between the creatures. That's why even today, the lion hates the monkey, and the cat despises the mouse.

Acinonyx *(cheetah)*

THE OLDEST RECOVERED fossils of true cats date back 18 million years. These cats evolved into the three main cat groups: *Acinonyx* (cheetah), *Panthera* (great cats), and *Felis* (small cats). From the *Felis* group came the wildcat, which inhabited areas of Europe, Asia, and Africa. It is the African wildcat that is the granddaddy of all domestic varieties. This sand-colored tabby became domesticated about 3,500 years ago, trading a walk on the wild side for the "mousy" rewards found in the grain stores of Egypt.

CATS IN EGYPT

EARLY EGYPTIANS WERE quick to recognize the mystical powers of the cat and set the feline on a pedestal. About 950 B.C., a cat goddess called Bast (or Bastet) was worshiped in the city of Bubastis. Bast was typically depicted as a cat or as a human with the head of a cat, often holding a sacred rattle known as a *sistrum*. Bast was favored by the sun god Ra (or Re) and was identified with the life-giving warmth of the sun. She was also associated with good health, music and dancing, happiness, and pleasure and was a symbol of motherhood and fertility.

A temple was built in Bast's honor, and sacred cats were kept in high style in the temple. Each mew, tail swish, and whisker flick was interpreted by the priests as a message sent from the goddess. Cats were held in such reverence that killing a cat carried the death penalty. Following the passing of a household cat, the entire family would shave their eyebrows in mourning. Cats were then mummified and entombed.

"Cats were put into the world to disprove the dogma that all things were created to serve man."

—Paul Gray

TEN WAYS TO WORSHIP YOUR CAT

1. Ring the sacred jingle bell every morning.

2. Scatter kibble offerings throughout the home.

3. Announce to the dog that it has come to your attention that canines are an inferior species.

4. Relinquish control of your bed.

5. Remove warm towels from dryer. Leave on bed. Walk away.

6. Offer the off-limits guest chair as a scratching post.

7. Catnip always says "I love you."

8. Release live mice in the house.

9. A 20-minute back scratch (ears included) never hurts.

10. Bow and declare your eternal loyalty and servitude (as if this hasn't already occurred).

MUMMIFIED REMAINS

IN ANCIENT EGYPT, cats were often mummified and placed in their owners' tombs or buried in special cat cemeteries. The largest cache of mummified remains was found at Beni Hasan in 1889. Hundreds of thousands of mummified cat bodies were discovered there.

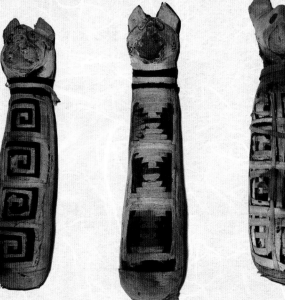

The bodies were treated with preservatives, then carefully wrapped in sheets of linen. The final outer covering was made of cloth, papyrus, or palm leaves. Cloth or palm leaves were attached to form upright ears, and feline faces were painted on the covering. Sometimes two colors were woven together in the outer covering to represent a cat's coat pattern. This sacred ceremony prepared the Egyptians' beloved cats for their life in the next world.

"**P**eople that hate cats will come
back as mice in their next life."

—Faith Resnick

 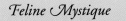

WILD TO MILD: THE AFRICAN WILDCAT

THE AFRICAN WILDCAT *(felis silvestris lybica)* is the predecessor to today's domestic cat. The small wildcats (ranging from about 8 to 11 pounds) arrived in Egypt about 5,000 years ago. Egyptians stored vast quantities of grain that attracted mice and other vermin—ample prey for the wildcat. The Egyptians were happy to have the cats to control the vermin population— and so began the kinship between human and cat.

After cohabitating with humans, the wildcat began to show changes in both temperament and appearance. Its personality became more docile, and the camouflage coat—no longer needed—morphed into today's tabby pattern.

Today, some wildcats are still found in deserts, savannas, woodlands, and forests throughout the Middle East and much of Africa. There, they exist much as they always have, preying on rodents, birds, and small reptiles.

Medieval legend says the devil tried to mimic God and create a man; instead a sorry, skinless creature appeared—the first cat. St. Peter took pity on the pathetic beast and gave the cat her only priceless possession: a fur coat.

"*In the beginning, God created man, but seeing him so feeble, He gave him the cat.*"
—WARREN ECKSTEIN

FELINE FORECASTERS

OVER THE AGES, cats have been used as seers to predict the weather, good fortune, and tragedy. The Egyptian word for cat is *mau*, meaning *to see*, or *seer*. Cats' eyes, which glow in the moonlight, were thought to hold second sight.

The Irish believed if kitty lay with her paws stretched out in front of her, a storm was on the way. Sailors believed a cat carried "a gale in its tail" that could be released at will. A cat on a ship playing with her tail or even a dangling rope was believed to be stirring up winds.

According to folklore, calico cats have the gift of second sight. Burmese cats were housed as oracles in Burmese temples. Tricolor cats were believed to protect the house where they lived from being destroyed by fire.

> "**I**f a cat washes her face over her ear,
> 'tis a sign the weather will be fine and clear."
> —ENGLISH PROVERB

*T*HE EGYPTIAN VENERATION of cats was well known throughout the world—and sometimes used to an enemy's advantage. At the Battle at Pelusium in 525 B.C., Persian soldiers shielded themselves with cats as they marched on the Egyptians, who feared killing even one of the sacred animals and were thereby defeated.

*"**W**hen a cat died, a wise Egyptian tried to be some-place else so that he couldn't be accused of its murder."*
—HERODOTUS

A BRIDGE BETWEEN WORLDS

CATS WERE THOUGHT to serve as a bridge between this world and the next. When members of the royal house of Siam were buried, a favorite cat was entombed alive with them. The roof of the tomb contained small holes, and if the cat managed to escape, the priests believed the human soul had passed into the cat's body. These venerated cats were then cared for in the temple. When the cats finally died, they conducted the human soul into paradise.

When King Prajadhipok of Siam (now Thailand) was crowned in 1925, a cat took its rightful place in the coronation procession to represent the prior ruler, King Rama VI.

"**A** cat may look at a king."

—ENGLISH PROVERB

King Prajadhipok

TRIM—FIRST CAT AROUND THE WORLD

AGLOSSY 12-POUND black cat with four white feet and a white star on his chest, Trim was the first cat to tour the globe and circumnavigate Australia. Trim was born at sea on a ship called *Roundabout* in 1799 and became the beloved cat of explorer Matthew Flinders (1774–1814), famous in his own right for being the first person to circumnavigate Australia—as well as name it.

Raised at sea, Trim demonstrated no fear of the water. He was an adept swimmer, and if he ever fell overboard while perusing the slippery deck, crew members would simply throw him a rope so he could scurry up to the safety of the ship.

After four happy years of adventures, 1803 marked the last year Trim set sail with Matthew Flinders. Sailing for England aboard the ship *Cumberland*, the pair were shipwrecked on a coral reef in the Indian Ocean. Matthew Flinders and Trim were rescued but imprisoned on the French island of Mauritius, where Flinders was held as a spy. After two weeks of captivity, Trim went missing and was presumed dead. Flinders was nearly inconsolable. Later in life, Flinders wrote, "I can never speak of cats without a sentiment of regret for my poor Trim, the favourite of all our ship's company."

A statue of Trim looking up at the statue of his master, Matthew Flinders, was erected in Sydney in 1995.

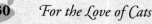

Statue of Trim

"*There is no more intrepid explorer than a kitten.*"

—JULES CHAMPFLEURY

CATS OUT OF EGYPT

ALTHOUGH THE FIRST domestic cats in ancient Egypt were jealously guarded, some were smuggled out of the country (under penalty of death to the smuggler). The species soon spread throughout the world. Domestic cats reached India around 2000 B.C. From India, the cat traveled to China, Japan, Greece, and finally Europe. Sailors traveling to the Middle East inadvertently brought back rats on their ships. To combat the rodents, cats were invited along for the ride, and the ships' cats were consequently distributed around the world.

CAT FACT:

Cats are not indigenous to the island of Cyprus (Mediterranean Sea), yet remains of cats, humans, and mice dating back more than 8,000 years have been found there together.

In Greek mythology, the sun god Apollo created the lion to frighten his sister Artemis, goddess of the moon. In return, Artemis created the cat, a miniature form of the lion meant to ridicule her brother.

"A cat is a lion in a jungle of small bushes."

—Indian Proverb

"Every morning in Africa, a gazelle wakes up. It knows it must run faster than the fastest lion or it will be killed. Every morning a lion wakes up. It knows that it must outrun the slowest gazelle or it will starve to death. It doesn't matter whether you are a lion or a gazelle, when the sun comes up, you'd better be running."

—Serengeti Proverb

"**O**f all God's creatures, there is only one that cannot be made slave of the leash. That one is the cat. If man could be crossed with the cat it would improve man, but it would deteriorate the cat."

—MARK TWAIN

Good-Luck Charms

Times change and eras roll by, but one constant is the role of the feline as talisman. Civilizations, governments, and individuals have all believed in the power of cats to see the future, heal, portend good tidings, or foreshadow bad luck. Below is a brief list of common "good luck" beliefs about cats through the ages:

- The ancient Chinese believed placing cat figurines on the outside of their huts and hanging pictures of felines indoors would hold poverty and bad luck at bay.

- Russian peasants placed cats in the cribs of newborns because they believed the cat would drive evil spirits away from the child.

- Buddhists believed that light-color cats ensured there would always be silver in the home and dark-color cats would keep them rich in gold.

- Many cultures thought cats' ability to see in the dark gave them the ability to detect—and chase away—evil spirits.

"**S**ome people say that cats are sneaky, evil, and cruel. True, and they have many other fine qualities as well."

—Missy Dizick

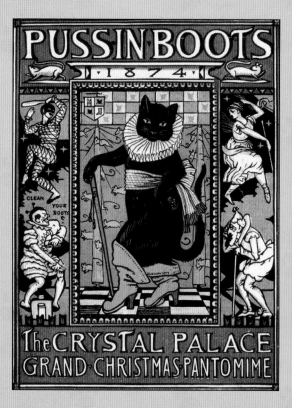

*T*HE ANCIENT STORY of Puss in Boots is best known from the Charles Perrault fairy-tale collection but may be of Arabic or even Sanskrit origin. It recounts the tale of a young but poor man who gains wealth, a title, and the king's daughter as his bride with the aid of a magical puss's trickery.

THE GODS WERE once disputing whether it was possible for a living being to change its nature. Jupiter said "Yes," but Venus said "No." So, to try the question, Jupiter turned a cat into a maiden, and gave her to a young man for a wife. The wedding was duly performed and the young couple sat down to the wedding feast. "See," said Jupiter, to Venus, "how becomingly she behaves. Who could tell that yesterday she was but a cat? Surely her nature is changed?"

"Wait a minute," replied Venus, and she let loose a mouse into the room. No sooner did the bride see this than she jumped up from her seat and tried to pounce upon the mouse.

"Ah, you see," said Venus, "nature will out." —AESOP'S FABLES

FROM FRIEND TO FOE:
THE PERSECUTED CAT

THE EARLY MIDDLE AGES brought an end to the cat's truce with Christianity. Threatened by symbols of pagan religions, the church denounced cats as profane. By the thirteenth century, cats were associated with devil worship, sorcery, and every evil imaginable—they became scapegoats at every turn. Satan was said to roam the earth in the guise of a black cat. Witches, it was reported, rode their cats to meet with the devil. Although some people superstitiously kept and protected black cats, believing this courtesy to Satan's favored animal would keep him off their back and help them prosper, thousands of cats were tortured and killed in the name of religion.

Nature, perhaps, evened the score by sending the Black Plague through Europe. Carried by fleas on rats, the disease ran rampant; the elimination of cats had enabled rats to populate the streets unchecked. More than one quarter of Europe's population fell to the plague before it was over. However, the epidemic was the beginning of the end of the cat's suffering, as people recognized cats were needed to control the rat population. By the end of the seventeenth century, cats were restored to their rightful place as popular pets in the home.

"*Ah! Cats are a mysterious kind of folk.
There is more passing in their minds than we
are aware of. It comes no doubt from their
being too familiar with warlocks and witches.*"

—SIR WALTER SCOTT

CATS IN ASIA

CATS ARRIVED IN China around 1000 B.C. There, felines were unfortunately linked with poverty, the thought being that well-run farms should not have rats and therefore had no need for cats. The cat's reputation in China was further tarnished when it was said that the cat and snake were the only two animals who did not weep at Buddha's death.

The feline fared better in Japan where Buddhist monks first introduced domestic cats around A.D. 600. All levels of Japanese society considered the cat sacred and revered. One wind god in ancient Japan was believed to take on the form of a cat and slash open the sky with its claws to bring rain. In addition, the Japanese used cats to safeguard their nation's most valuable commodity of the time—silkworm farms.

THE MANEKI NEKO OR "BECKONING CAT"

IN A POPULAR Japanese legend, a priest at a seventeenth-century temple in Tokyo chides the temple's cat for neglecting the temple, which was looking shoddy in appearance.

A few days later, a local lord, Naotaka, sought protection from heavy rains under a tree near the temple. It was then he noticed the temple's cat, Tama, beckoning him inside the temple. As the lord dashed from the tree's shelter toward the temple, the tree was struck by lightning. The grateful lord adopted the temple for his family and with his influence, the priest and temple prospered. Tama was eventually buried at Goutokuji's cat cemetery with much respect and honor, and it is from her actions that the popular Japanese Maneki Neko, or "beckoning cat" tradition was begun.

The Japanese Maneki Neko, or beckoning cat figurine, is a good-luck symbol popular even today. The beckoning cat is always adorned with a red ribbon around its neck, holding a bell on the front. Tricolored figurines are among the most popular, but Maneki Neko come in all varieties. Other popular colors are white, representing purity, and black, thought to ward off evil. Often one of the lucky cat's paws is raised—tradition says a raised left paw invites customers, while a raised right paw welcomes fortune.

Vampire Cats

Today, when we think of vampires, our minds turn immediately to bats. However, it wasn't until Bram Stoker's *Dracula*, published in 1897, that there was any association between vampires and bats. According to tradition in sixteenth- and seventeenth-century Europe, vampires were either wolves or cats.

Tales of cats as vampires date back to Adam. The ancient belief that cats steal breath from babies arose from Hebrew mythology. According to legend, Adam's first wife, Lilith, fled Eden and became a vampire who could assume the form of a huge black cat called El Broosha. Human newborns were supposedly El Broosha's favorite prey.

MYTH VS. FACT:

SO WHY *DO* CATS approach babies? One thought is cats are attracted to the smell of a baby's milky breath. Also, cats are so intensely alert to change that some bump noses with a baby if they notice something different. Numerous cats are on record for alerting parents when a baby has a high fever or has stopped breathing. For those who need additional reassurance, nose bumps from felines are a sign of affection, not breath stealing!

SIAMESE CATS WERE first seen more than 200 years ago and get their name from the country of Siam (now Thailand). These long, lithe cats love to climb and scrabble, earning themselves the nickname "spider-monkey cats."

According to legend, these cats guarded their masters' jewels in the palaces of Siam. They wore bracelets on their neck, giving them a long, elegant neck; draped necklaces over their shoulders, creating an upright, regal stance; and wore rings on their tails, adding a kink in the tail. Another story to explain the kink tells how the Siamese tied a knot in her tail to remind her of something—which she can't remember to this day.

A Siamese's eyes are sometimes crossed. Legend holds that a Siamese ancestor stared too long and hard at Buddha's golden goblet, thereby explaining away the crossed eyes.

Another legend describes how the Siamese earned the "temple mark"— two distinct darker smudges across the back—found on highbred cats. The story goes that an unknown holy being once picked up a Siamese cat and left the shadow of his hands forever on Siamese descendants.

Siamese cats are known for being wonderfully affectionate but also demanding. They have a highly developed language and are known to be the most talkative of the breeds. Siamese came to the United States in the late 1800s and remain, with good reason, one of the most popular breeds today.

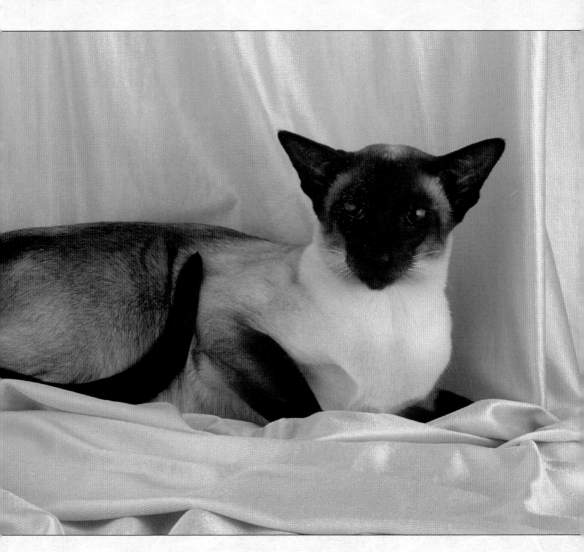

"*I believe cats to be spirits come to earth. A cat, I am sure, could walk on a cloud without coming through.*"

—JULES VERNE

Chapter Two
Famous Felines

Cats have kept good company
through the ages. They've also earned
their own place in the spotlight.

Cat Fanciers

- Anne Frank shared cramped quarters with a white-socked cat named Boche.

- Winston Churchill kept a succession of cats, including Nelson, Margate, and a marmalade cat named Jock.

- At one time, Florence Nightingale had more than 60 Persians whom she named after public figures, such as Bismarck, Gladstone, and Disraeli.

- The prophet Mohammed was very fond of a little cat he called Muezza. Mohammed is reported to have cut off his sleeve rather than disturb the cat, which was sleeping on it.

Florence Nightingale

Feline Foes

Dwight Eisenhower

- Johannes Brahms refused to go near cats.

- President Dwight Eisenhower banished cats from the White House and gave standing orders that cats trespassing on White House grounds should be shot on sight.

- Alexander the Great despised cats (perhaps making him not so great).

- Shakespeare had nothing good to say (or write) about cats.

- Napoleon Bonaparte suffered from a clinical cat phobia and was said to become hysterical when faced with a feline.

DID YOU KNOW…

A person who loves cats is called an *ailurophile;* people who fear cats are known as *ailurophobes.*

$\mathcal{W}$HEN ASKED WHY he had not taken his beloved kitten, Patsy, along for company on his historic 1927 transatlantic flight, Charles Lindbergh explained that he didn't want to risk his cat's life on such a dangerous journey.

"The cat is nature's Beauty."

—FRENCH PROVERB

"The dog may be wonderful prose,
but only the cat is poetry."

—FRENCH PROVERB

Famous Cats in Literature

- The Black Cat from Edgar Allan Poe's short story of the same name

- "The Cat that Walked by Himself" in Rudyard Kipling's *Just So Stories*

- Tom Kitten; Tom's mother, Mrs. Tabitha Twitchit; and his siblings Moppet and Mittens, all from stories by Beatrix Potter

- Crookshanks, Hermione Granger's cat in the *Harry Potter* series

- Pixel in *The Cat Who Walks Through Walls* by Robert A. Heinlein

- *The Cat in the Hat* by Dr. Seuss

More Cat Fanciers

- Bob Barker, host of *The Price is Right*

- Ernest Hemingway, writer

- Betty White, actor and animal activist

- Brigitte Bardot, actor

- Abraham Lincoln

DID YOU KNOW...

Abraham Lincoln rescued three orphaned kittens during a visit to General Grant's camp during the Civil War.

DR. SEUSS

THEODOR GEISEL, better known to legions of fans as "Dr. Seuss," wrote *The Cat in the Hat* because he felt primers for beginning readers should contain fun and imaginative reading material. In a 1981

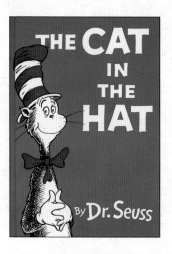

interview, Dr. Seuss explained that the title for the book came from his desire to rhyme— the first two words that he could find were *cat* and *hat*. It took the beloved author more than nine months to write the book. The task was made more difficult because Seuss had to select text from an approved list (supplied by his publisher to parallel a reading program taught in schools) of only 223 words.

Where Did the Cheshire Cat Get Its Grin?

RUMOR HAS IT that the inspiration for the Cheshire Cat in *Alice's Adventures in Wonderland* came from author Lewis Carroll's childhood. His father was a rector at a church that featured a cat carving. From the viewpoint of a child, all that can often be seen of the carving is the huge grin on the cat's face.

DID YOU KNOW...

The young girl on whom the character Alice of *Alice's Adventures in Wonderland* is based had a cat named Dinah.

"*Perhaps it is because cats do not live by human patterns, do not fit themselves into prescribed behavior, that they are so united to creative people.*"

—Andre Norton

Cats in Advertising

🐾 In the 1890s, Hoyt's Cologne featured a cat and kittens on advertising cards.

🐾 Coca-Cola ran a popular 1920s ad that featured a white cat lapping milk from a blue bowl as her stylish owner enjoyed a Coke.

In the 1920s, Black Cat was the name of a stove polish.

Esso used an ad slogan that read: "The Esso Tiger—Put A Tiger in Your Tank!"

Kitty Kat shoes were produced by the James Clark Leather Co. of St. Louis.

Cigar brands named after felines include: Two Toms, Our Kitties, Cats, Pussy, Mr. Thomas, Old Tom, Tabby, Me-Ow, and White Cat.

KELLOGG'S CATS

KELLOGG'S FIRST FELINE advertising success came along in 1914, when they used a picture of a child holding a gray cat alongside the slogan "For Kiddies not Kitties" to market Toasted Corn Flakes.

But their big hit came in 1952 when Tony the Tiger came bounding onto the scene as the spokesperson (er, spokes*cat*) for Kellogg's Sugar Frosted Flakes (later, just "Frosted Flakes"). Tony was originally one of four animated creatures in a campaign that included Katy the Kangaroo, Newt the Gnu, and Elmo the Elephant. But the blue-nosed, orange-and-black striped Tony—along with his trademark roar, "They're Grrrreat!"—quickly vaulted to solo status as the king feline of the cereal world.

Tony the Tiger says, "I'd stalk a mile for...

Kellogg's Sugar Frosted Flakes"

Everybody's stalking about 'em
There hasn't been so much conversation about a "cereal" since the days of "The Perils of Pauline." So you've probably heard that these big flakes of corn, covered all over with Kellogg's secret sugar frosting, are "Gr-r-reat" for breakfast or snacks. But why talk about Kellogg's Sugar Frosted Flakes? Stalk down to your grocer's and get the *inside* story right out of the box. C'mon, let's race!

 For the Love of Cats

*T*HE NORMAN ROCKWELL of the 1890s, French graphic artist Théophile-Alexandre Steinlen's drawings of cats were seen all over Paris in advertisements and posters. His most popular painting was titled "Chat Noir." The popularity of Steinlen's cat illustrations is as strong today as it was then.

"**W**hat greater gift than the love of a cat?"

—CHARLES DICKENS

"The problem with cats is that they get the same exact look whether they see a moth or an axe murderer."

—Paula Poundstone

IT WAS A DARK AND STORMY NIGHT...

Perhaps due to their feline mystique or their wily ways, cats have always been popular in "who-done-it" mystery novels, usually solving the crime despite the "help" of a bumbling human partner. Some "hair-raising" mystery books with cat protagonists:

🐾 *The Cat Who...* series by Lilian Jackson Braun now numbers 28 books featuring detective James Qwilleran and his two Siamese cats Koko and Yum Yum.

🐾 The *Felidae* novels by Akif Pirinçci feature Francis as the feline detective.

🐾 Carole Nelson Douglas has brought fame to Midnight Louie and his daughter, Midnight Louise, in a series of novels that follow amateur human sleuth and cat lover Temple Barr.

🐾 Author Rita Mae Brown coauthors her books with her cat Sneaky Pie Brown as they write about feline sleuth Mrs. Murphy.

🐾 Shirley Rousseau Murphy's feline investigator, Joe Grey, gets help from his fellow talking cats, who call in tips to the local police.

🐾 Marian Babson uses various feline finders in her novels.

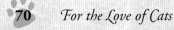 *For the Love of Cats*

"*I* *wish I could write as* *mysterious as a cat.*"
—Edgar Allan Poe

Film Spotlight:

"I'm as jumpy as a cat on a hot tin roof!"

—Elizabeth Taylor as Maggie "The Cat" in the 1958 movie of the Tennessee Williams play *Cat on a Hot Tin Roof*

Cat with a Bird in Its Jaws *by Pablo Picasso*

IN THE SPRING OF 1904, a young Pablo Picasso moved to Montmartre, the famous artists' section of Paris. Picasso took in a stray cat, whom he named Minou. The cat watched Picasso paint during his Blue period. Eventually, unable to sell enough paintings to feed even himself, Picasso turned Minou out to the streets to fend for herself. However, Minou did not abandon the painter. Instead, to Picasso's surprise, she returned that evening with a sausage, which she laid at the door to share with Picasso. Touched, Picasso welcomed the little black-and-white cat back into his home where she lived out her days.

Cats in the White House

🐾 Bill Clinton, the 42nd president of the United States, allowed First Cat Socks free rein at the White House.

🐾 President Coolidge's cat Timmie was the ultimate diplomat, encouraging improved species relations. Timmie allowed the White House canary, Caruso, to strut up and down his back and even to snuggle between his shoulders for a nap.

🐾 According to William Herndon, Lincoln's biographer, whenever the 16th president grew weary from the burdens of office, he would "stop thought and get down and play with a little … kitten to recover."

🐾 President Rutherford B. Hayes's cat was the first Siamese to arrive in the United States.

🐾 Susan Ford, daughter of former President Gerald Ford, kept a beautiful Siamese named Shan.

🐾 Another first daughter, Amy Carter, lived with a beloved Siamese kitty named Misty Malarky Ying Yang.

Amy Carter and Misty Malarky Ying Yang

First Cat Socks

AFTER 12 "CATLESS" YEARS at the White House,
First Cat Socks took the country by storm.
Socks was given to President Bill Clinton's daughter
Chelsea by one of her elementary school friends when he
was just a kitten. A distinguished black-and-white cat,
Socks had his own newsletter and fan club.

 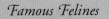

DO YOU MIND?

CATS OFTEN APPEARED as companions in the portraits of painters, including the works of Pierre-Auguste Renoir, Henri Rousseau, and Pierre Bonnard. But before them, Gottfried Mind (1767–1814) was the first painter to specialize in portraits of cats themselves rather than their owners. Mind always worked with his favorite cat nearby and her kittens draped over his shoulder. In 1809, an outbreak of rabies resulted in the destruction of all cats in the city. Mind managed to hide and save his beloved cat Minette.

Other Famous Painters of the Feline Form:

- Albrecht Dürer
- Paul Klee
- Francisco de Goya
- Leonardo da Vinci
- Edward Lear
- Alexander Calder
- Gustave Courbet
- Marc Chagall
- Eugène Delacroix

- Jean-Auguste-Dominique Ingres
- Pierre-Auguste Renoir
- Andrew Wyeth
- Henri de Toulouse-Lautrec
- Paul Gauguin
- Édouard Manet
- Suzanne Valadon
- Antoine Watteau
- Rembrandt van Rijn

"The smallest feline is a masterpiece."
—Leonardo da Vinci

May Belfort *by Henri de Toulouse- Lautrec*

CATERWAULING

- One of the most famous pieces of "cat music" is Edward Lear's verse *The Owl and the Pussycat,* set to music by Stravinsky.

- Rossini composed "Duetto Buffo Dei Due Gatti," a duet for two female singers who vocalize solely on the word *meow.*

- Domenico Scarlatti's "Cat Fugue" was inspired by his feline running over the piano keyboard. The cat's paw-tread became the underlying theme in the piece.

- Tchaikovsky's *Sleeping Beauty* ballet includes a beautiful pas de deux for two fairy-tale cat figures.

"*There are two means of refuge from the miseries of life: music and cats.*"

—ALBERT SCHWEITZER

Big Cats in Literature for Little People

* Aslan the Lion in *The Lion, the Witch, and the Wardrobe* by C. S. Lewis

* Bagheera the panther and Shere Kahn the tiger in Rudyard Kipling's *The Jungle Book*

The Cowardly Lion

Tigger

* The Cowardly Lion from *The Wonderful Wizard of Oz*

* Tigger in *Winnie the Pooh*

Cats on the Big Screen

- Figaro was the name of the cat featured in Disney's *Pinocchio*.

- Mr. Bigglesworth, Dr. Evil's cat from the *Austin Powers* films, was a tribute to Blofeld's unnamed cat from the *James Bond* movies. Both a Persian and Sphynx play the lap-hugging role of Mr. Bigglesworth.

- The movie *Alien* included a cat named Jones.

- Cat was Holly Golightly's (played by Audrey Hepburn) feline roommate in *Breakfast at Tiffany's*.

- Cosmic Creepers was a black cat in Disney's 1971 film, *Bedknobs and Broomsticks*.

- Scat Cat, Maria, and others join in the animated cast of Disney's *The Aristocats*. Scat Cat was modeled after Louis Armstrong, who was

The Aristocats

originally scheduled to do the voice. Replacement Scatman Crothers was instructed: "Pretend you're Satchmo."

- Pyewacket played the magical cat in the romantic comedy *Bell, Book, and Candle.*

- The film version of *Stuart Little* featured Snowball, the cat.

- In the opening scenes of *The Godfather,* Marlon Brando held a small, unnamed cat on his lap.

- Antonio Banderas gave voice to Puss-in-Boots, the catnip-carrying cat in *Shrek 2.*

The Godfather

FILM SPOTLIGHT:

The first cat to appear on the silver screen was a gray stray named Pepper. She stole the hearts of silent-film viewers when she starred with Charlie Chaplin, Fatty Arbuckle, and the Keystone Kops.

GLAMOUR PUSS VERSUS GREMLIN

Persian

FOR THOSE SEEKING the ultimate in luxury lap-cats, look no further than the long-furred, fluffy Persian. Once a cat associated with aristocracy, the Persian is now recognized as the most popular breed in the world. In contrast to the megalomaniac roles Hollywood directors seem wont to cast them in, these quiet-voiced, laid-back felines are happiest when allowed to relax in secluded spots and watch the world pass by.

FILM SPOTLIGHT:

Mr. Tinkles from the Warner Brothers movie *Cats & Dogs* is a white Persian on a power trip. Mr. Tinkles considers anything other than total domination of the canine species (and possibly the human species, while he's at it) to be unworthy of his attention.

Sphynx

ALTHOUGH THEIR NAME conjures up images of ancient Egypt and pyramids, Sphynx—also known as Hot Water Bottle Cats—hail from hearty Canada. Contrary to popular belief, the cats are not completely hairless but are often covered with a fine down that feels like warm suede. They also grow small tufts of hair on the tips of their tails and at the base of their ears. The cats are meant to be strictly indoor cats, given their lack of natural protection against the elements. Although Sphynx have yet to catch on as a popular pet, their soft voice and gentle ways endear them to their owners.

Film Spotlight:

Now known as Si and Am, the twin Siamese cats in the hit Disney film *Lady and the Tramp* were originally named Nip and Tuck.

COPY CAT:

FOR YEARS, Leo the Lion roared as the mascot for Metro-Goldwyn-Mayer (MGM) film studio. In good fun, owners of MTM (Mary Tyler Moore) Enterprises, Inc., decided to parody the famous lion by using a small orange kitten as their mascot. Hoping to capture a head-on meow, a camera crew spent a frustrating day filming a group of kittens who refused to cooperate by "roaring" at the camera. Ready to call it quits and search for another mascot, an editor finally realized he could reverse a piece of film in which one of the kittens yawned, thereby producing the desired "roar."

Do You Remember...

❧ The Pink Panther

❧ Disney's 1978 film *The Cat from Outer Space*

❧ Sylvester "Sufferin' Succotash!" of Warner Brothers fame

❧ The *Thundercats* cartoon series

❧ Battlecat (from *He-Man and the Masters of the Universe*)

❧ Toonces the Driving Cat from *Saturday Night Live*

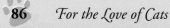

SOLICITOUS FELINES

- Charles Dickens's cat snuffed out candles with her paws when she wanted attention.

- When Edgar Allan Poe's wife, Virginia, was sick, the family was so poor they couldn't afford enough coal to keep the house warm. So the Poes' cat, Catterina, would curl up on Virginia's chest, acting as a blanket as she warmed Virginia with her body heat. Because of Catterina, Virginia was kept warm during her illness.

"**A**uthors like cats because they are such quiet, lovable, wise creatures, and cats like authors for the same reasons."

—Robertson Davies

"**C**ats are dangerous companions for writers because cat watching is a near-perfect method of writing avoidance."

—Dan Greenburg

Musical Cats

Cat purrs are music to any cat lover's ears, and the furry feline has inspired her share of musical hits throughout the years.

- 🐾 "Cat Black (the Wizard's Hat)" by T. Rex

- 🐾 "Tommy the Cat" by Primus

- 🐾 "Leave My Kitten Alone" by Little Willie John

- 🐾 "What's New Pussycat?" by Tom Jones

- 🐾 *Year of the Cat* by Al Stewart

- 🐾 *Cheshire Cat* by blink-182

- 🐾 "Stray Cat Strut" by The Stray Cats

- 🐾 "Cat's in the Cradle" by Harry Chapin

- 🐾 "Black Cat" by Janet Jackson

- 🐾 *CATS*, the musical by Lord Andrew Lloyd Webber

LORD ANDREW LLOYD WEBBER'S CATS

Nursery rhymes written by T.S. Eliot were published in 1939 as *Old Possum's Book of Practical Cats*. The book is the basis for the enormously successful musical *CATS*. The now well-known cats include:

- The Old Gumbie Cat

- Growltiger

- Rum Tum Tugger

- Mungojerrie and Rumpelteazer

- Old Deuteronomy

- Mr. Mistoffelees

- Macavity: The Mystery Cat

- Bustopher Jones: The Cat about Town

- Skimbleshanks: The Railway Cat

If not for a bit of kitty providence, *CATS* may not have been written. The T.S. Eliot verses upon which the production was based lacked a narrative thread. Then Eliot's widow gave Webber an unpublished handwritten verse omitted from the original children's book. Called "Grizabella, the Glamour Cat," the verse lent the production the central character it needed.

Facts About *CATS:*

- *CATS* first pounced on the stage in 1981.

- There are 36 feline characters.

- September 28, 1994, marked the 5,000th Broadway performance of *CATS*, putting it in league with *A Chorus Line* and *Oh! Calcutta!*

- In 1983, *CATS* won seven Tony Awards including best musical, best lighting, and best costumes.

- *CATS* has the distinction of being the longest continuously touring musical in American theater history. Its Broadway run ended on September 10, 2000.

- *CATS* has been seen on 5 continents and in 26 countries.

"Cats, like men, are flatterers."

—William S. Landor

Do You Remember...

🐾 Henrietta Pussycat and Daniel Striped Tiger from *Mister Rogers' Neighborhood*

🐾 The pet lion named Kitty Kat from the 1960s TV series *The Addams Family*

🐾 How the puppet space-alien ALF on the 1980s TV series kept trying to eat the family cat, Lucky

🐾 Lucifer, the cat in Disney's *Cinderella*

🐾 Snagglepuss, the pink talking lion of Hanna-Barbera fame

Lucifer

MORRIS THE 9LIVES CAT

The wise-cracking Morris first entered American homes in 1968 after professional animal handler Bob Martwick rescued him from a Chicago animal shelter 20 minutes before he was to be put down. Morris quickly moved from 9Lives spokescat to cultural icon, running twice for president (1988 and 1992); appearing in movies with Burt Reynolds; and on *Oprah*, the *Today* show, and *Lifestyles of the Rich and Famous*, among others. He also found time to pen three books.

Del Monte reinstated the Morris campaign in 2005, and the search for a new Morris was on. Veteran animal trainer Rose Ordile was enlisted to help search the nation's shelters.

Once they found a new Morris, it took about six months of training before he was ready for the commercial shoot.

Movie sets often use a team of cats for different shots. However, since there is only one Morris, each commercial is shot over several days. There's a lot of setup involved for each take, whether it's a rub or pounce or Morris staring languidly into the camera.

When not shooting commercials, Ordile and Morris tour the nation promoting pet adoption, responsible pet ownership, and pet health.

An Intimate Biography by Mary Daniels

Talk about celebrity—the life and times of Morris have been chronicled in his very own biography. Written by Mary Daniels, An Intimate Biography *was published in 1974.*

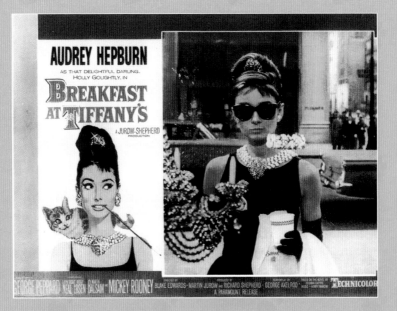

THE FIRST Picture Animal Top Star of the Year award (PATSY) was won in 1951 by an orange tabby named Orangey. Orangey won top acting awards for the title role of "Rhubarb" in a story about a cat who inherits a million dollars. Orangey went on to receive a second PATSY award in the role of "Cat" in the 1961 film *Breakfast at Tiffany's* with the only slightly less well-known Audrey Hepburn. Orangey won more show business awards than any other cat.

"**H**er conscious tail her joy declared,
The fair round face, the snowy beard,
The velvet of her paws,
Her coat, that with the tortoise views,
Her ears of jet, and emerald eyes,
She saw; and purred applause."

—THOMAS GRAY, EXCERPT FROM *THE TEMPTED CAT*

Famous Felines

IN THE ANIMAL film industry a number of cats typically compete for roles. In a feature film, a crew works with a team of cats—four or five cats usually play the part of one.

For "star qualities," kitty must learn to "hit the mark," touch a prop, and hiss or meow on command. One former TV star, Princess Kitty, could perform more than 70 tricks on command, including slam-dunking a cat-size basketball.

FILM SPOTLIGHT:

Data's cat, Spot, on the popular series *Star Trek: The Next Generation* was first played by a Somali cat named Liberty Valance and then by two look-alike orange tabby cats named Brandy and Monster.

Do You Remember...

- Azrael, the pet of cunning Gargamel on the TV show *The Smurfs*

- Black Pete, the nemesis of first Mickey Mouse and then Goofy

- Fritz the Cat

- Heathcliff, an average-Joe cat

- Felix the Cat—the first cartoon cat to appear in film in the 1920s

Felix the Cat

Cat Fact:

WILLIAM HANNA and Joseph Barbera of Hanna-Barbera fame created what was perhaps the most successful cat and mouse team ever with the 1939 release of *Tom & Jerry*. The dueling duo went on to appear in more than 200 films.

Cats that Make Us Laugh:

🐾 Bill the cat, close friend of Opus the penguin, from *Bloom County* and *Opus*. Bill is known for his riveting "Oop aack" dialogue as well as a propensity for um, well . . . throwing up. Bill also ran (unsuccessfully) several times for president on the National Radical Meadow Party Ticket.

🐾 Catbert, the evil Human Resources director from the popular *Dilbert* comic strip. Catbert enjoys taunting employees by holding an organizational chart over their heads and making them leap for it.

Catbert, as seen in this original cartoon cell

🐾 Snowball I (deceased white cat) and Snowball II (black cat) owned by Lisa Simpson on *The Simpsons*.

🐾 Hobbes, Calvin's beloved stuffed tiger from the comic strip *Calvin and Hobbes*. We should all be fortunate enough to find such a friend.

🐾 Garfield of *Garfield* fame.

Garfield with Jim Davis, his creator

GARFIELD: AMERICA'S FAVORITE FAT FELINE

Garfield's Loves:
lasagna

Arlene

naps

mealtimes

his sunbeam

his teddy bear,
    Pooky

Jon

Garfield's Dislikes:
diets

Nermal, the
    world's cutest
    kitten

alarm clocks

spiders

Odie (but not
    really)

HELLO KITTY

HELLO KITTY IS the popular cartoon creation of the Sanrio Company of Japan. Initially, the white, mouthless female kitten from London didn't have a name. However, the instant outpouring of love and respect for her sayings ("Hello Kitty says you can never have too many friends!") created a groundswell that turned the small cat into a global celebrity.

Hello Kitty typically sports a small red bow beneath her left ear but can sometimes be seen with a flower there instead. She has no mouth; the explanation offered by Sanrio is that there is no need for one because Hello Kitty always speaks from the heart. Some have equated Hello Kitty with the traditional Japanese beckoning cat, the Maneki Neko.

OFFICIAL PROFILE OF HELLO KITTY

Name: Kitty White

Birthday: November 1, 1974

Blood type: A

Place of birth: Suburban London

Height: That of five apples

Weight: That of three apples

Good at: Baking cookies

Favorite food: Apple pie made by Mama (A.K.A. Mum or Mary)

Favorite word: "Friendship"

Collects: Small cute things like sweets, stars, goldfish, etc.

Best school subjects: English, music, and visual arts

Description: A bright and kind-hearted kitten. Very close to her twin sister Mimmy.

"**H**ello Kitty says you can never have too many friends!"

Who Is Catwoman?

CATWOMAN IS A DC Comics character hailing from the *Batman* series. Originally known as "The Cat" she was intended to be an antagonist for Batman. However, just like a real cat, her loyalties and motives were sometimes ambiguous, and she was known to abhor killing. Catwoman's "real" name is Selina Kyle, named after the ancient lunar deity Selene.

Julie Newmar played Catwoman for the first two seasons on TV, but Lee Meriwether replaced her for the movie, due to a scheduling conflict on Newmar's part. Eartha Kitt eventually replaced Newmar in the third season of the TV series.

Catwoman's costume has undergone numerous changes over the years. In the first season, she wore a theaterlike cat mask that covered her entire face. Later, she wore a dress, and soon after that she exchanged the dress for a bodysuit. The bodysuit was changed to green in the 1960s and a body-molding purple in the 1990s. The most popular catwoman suit of all time may be that worn by sultry actress Michelle Pfeiffer in the 1992 *Batman Returns* movie. *Catwoman* the movie, starring Halle Berry, was released in 2004, but the bikini-topped costume was generally agreed to look like something the cat dragged in.

Michelle Pfeiffer

HIT 'EM HIGH, HIT 'EM LOW, HIT 'EM TEAM—GO! GO! GO!

Sports Teams Named After Cats

Carolina Panthers

Detroit Lions

Jacksonville Jaguars

Cincinnati Bengals

"**T**he really great thing about cats is their endless variety. One can pick a cat to fit almost any kind of decor, color scheme, income, personality, mood. But under the fur; whatever color it may be, there still lies, essentially unchanged, one of the world's free souls."

—Eric Gurney

ERNEST HEMINGWAY HOME AND MUSEUM

WHEN ERNEST HEMINGWAY acquired a cat with six toes from a ship's captain he became very taken with his special new friend. Today, a colony of about 60 cats, many direct descendants from Papa Hemingway's first six-toed cat, live at the Ernest Hemingway Home and Museum on the island of Key West. The museum takes responsibility for the care and feeding of the felines, who vary in size, shape, and color. About half of the cats have extra toes, usually on their front feet. The extra toe has been described as looking like a thumb for the paw.

CAT FACT:

Polydactyl is the term used to refer to a cat with extra toes—the "Hemingway cats." A normal cat paw has five toes on the front and four in back. Extra toes appear due to a mutant gene, and it's quite common for a parent to pass the polydactyl trait down to offspring. Most polydactyl cats have only one or two extra toes, but occasionally groupings of up to three or four extra toes are found.

Helpful Humans

PRESIDENT CALVIN COOLIDGE had three cats: Timmie, Tiger, and Blacky. Tiger was a wanderer. One day when Tiger didn't come home, Coolidge asked a local radio station for help in locating his cat. The station broadcast Tiger's description and passed on the President's request to help find the cat. Tiger was soon discovered at the Navy building (perhaps trying to enlist?) and was returned to the grateful President.

Pussycat, Pussycat

Pussycat, pussycat, where have you been?
I've been to London to visit the Queen.
Pussycat, pussycat, what did you there?
I frightened a little mouse under her chair.

FAMOUS FELINE

White Heather, the black-and-white Persian doted upon by Queen Victoria of England (1819–1901), survived Victoria's death and was taken up by her successor King Edward VII.

Three Little Kittens

Three little kittens,
They lost their mittens,
And they began to cry,
Oh, mother, dear,
We sadly fear,
Our mittens we have lost.

Betty White has been a pet lover her whole life. She found a stunning black cat hanging out in her backyard shortly after her husband, Allen Ludden, passed away. In typical cat fashion, the feline vanished if White so much as looked at it. However, the cat seemed fascinated by Timmy, White's little black poodle. Eventually, the homeless cat started accepting food from Betty. Then one day the stray kitty followed Timmy inside. It took a long time to win the cat's trust, but Timmy eventually made friends with the black cat. Betty promptly adopted the feline and named him T.K. for Timmy's Kitty.

FAMOUS PEOPLE AND THEIR CATS

Warren Beatty: Cake

Cleopatra: Charmain

Yoko Ono: Charo

Walter Cronkite: Dancer

John Lennon: Elvis

Andy Warhol: Hester

Elizabeth Taylor:
    Jeepers Creepers

Jane Pauley: Meatball

Marilyn Monroe: Mitsou

Vanna White: Rhett Butler

Martha Stewart: Weeny

Mark Twain: Zoroaster

Martha Stewart and Weeny

Cats
remind us
that all works
of beauty
should be
admired.

SAMUEL CLEMENS, commonly known as Mark Twain, had a deep and abiding love and respect for cats and often referred to them in his writing. He gave his cats tongue-twisting monikers to help children practice pronunciation. At one time, he shared his house with cats named Buffalo Bill, Beelzebub, Blather-skite, and Apollinaris. Twain's property adjoined that of Harriet Beecher Stowe (author of *Uncle Tom's Cabin*), who also loved and cherished her cats. Since the two sets of felines often visited each other, the authors had the cats "write" letters to one another.

A Pox upon Him!

WILLIAM SHAKESPEARE'S WORK contained more than 40 references to cats. Unfortunately, none of them were complimentary. Shakespeare's view of the cat is summed up in *All's Well That Ends Well:* "I could endure anything but a cat. And now he's a cat to me … A pox upon him! For he is more and more a cat."

CHAPTER THREE

Roars and Purrs
Heard Around the World

*Cultures across the globe have stories, sayings,
festivals, and awards to celebrate the cat.
There is a universal love of all things feline.*

"Meow is like aloha—it can mean anything."

—Hank Ketchum

Do You Speak Cat?

Afrikaans	miaau		Hindi	mya:u, mya:u
Albanian	mjau		Hungarian	miau
Arabic (Algeria)	miaou miaou		Icelandic	mja'
Bengali	meu-meu		Indonesia	ngeong
Chinese (Mandarin)	miao miao		Italian	miao
Croatian	mijau		Japanese	nyaa
Danish	mjav		Korean	(n)ya-ong
Dutch	miauw		Norwegian	mjau
English	meow		Polish	miau
Finnish	miau, kurnau		Portuguese	miau
French	miaou		Spanish	miau
German	miau		Swedish	mjau
Greek	niaou		Thai	meow meow
Hebrew	miyau		Turkish	miyauv, miyauv

HAPPY CAT DAY!

CIRCLE AUGUST 15 on your calendar. That's the day author (and former "Mr. Artist" on the *Captain Kangaroo* show) Stuart Hample wants reserved for national "Cat Day." Hample is the author of *Happy Cat Day: A Manifesto for an Official Cat Holiday,* and he has created a Web site to further his cause. He's also pushing for the issuance of a Cat Day stamp.

AUGUST				1	2	3
4	5	6	7	8	9	10
11	12	13	14	15	16	17
18	19	20	21	22	23	24
25	26	27	28	29	30	31

Other (Unofficial) Cat Holidays:

JANUARY 22
- Answer Your Cat's Silly Questions Day

MAY 15
- Hug Your Cat Day

MAY 26
- Curl up with Your Cat Day (Britain)

JUNE
- Adopt a Shelter Cat Month

POLISH LEGEND HAS IT that a group of kittens were chasing butterflies along the river's edge when, in their exuberance, they fell into the water. Desperate to help yet unable to reach her offspring, the mother cat started crying.

Hearing her cries, the willows along the river's edge dipped their branches into the water. The kittens were able to grab hold and pull themselves up using the long branches.

Now every spring, the willow sprouts tiny buds of fur on her branches in remembrance of the kittens.

124   *For the Love of Cats*

PROVERBS FROM AROUND THE WORLD

"When the mouse laughs at the cat, there is a hole nearby."

—NIGERIAN

"You will always be lucky if you know
how to make friends with strange cats."

—COLONIAL

"I gave an order to a cat, and the cat gave it to its tail."

—CHINESE

"The cat who frightens the mice away
is as good as the cat who eats them."

—GERMAN

"A cat may go to a monastery, but she still remains a cat."

—ETHIOPIAN

"In a cat's eye, all things belong to cats."

—ENGLISH

Cats on Record

*I*N 1950, a determined kitten from Switzerland followed a group of hikers to the summit of the Matterhorn in the Swiss Alps—a climb of 14,691 feet.

"Life is either a daring adventure or nothing."
—HELEN KELLER

Little-Known Tidbits About Little-Known Cats

🐾 According to Bushmen legend, the small black-footed cat of Africa is said to take down giraffes by pouncing at their necks.

🐾 The fishing cat of eastern Asia has partially webbed toes to aid in swimming.

Jaguarundi

🐾 There are reports of a wild cat known as the onza living in Mexico. The Aztecs called the cat Cuitlamiztli. Hunters claimed to have killed one of these legendary cats in 1986, but DNA determined that it was not genetically different from a cougar.

🐾 Take a good look: With its otter shape, the jaguarundi of South America is very good at swimming—and disguising itself. This rain-forest feline is reported to be the "least catlike" of cats.

Turkish Vans missed the memo that cats are supposed to hate water. They are referred to as the swimming cats since they often like to take a dip in the pool. Turkish Vans naturally love water. Originating in the Lake Van region of southeast Turkey, these cats were often seen paddling about. The people of the region prefer their Van cats to have a distinctive shoulder spot. They call this the "thumbprint of Allah," indicating that the cat has been blessed from heaven.

Dick Whittington

THE PANTOMIME STORY OF Dick Whittington and his cat is a British classic and has been told since the fifteenth century. Penniless Dick walked to London in search of fortune. He found work with a rich merchant and used his first earnings to buy a cat. When one of the merchant's trading vessels set sail, he asked all his servants to contribute something to sell. Poor Dick had only his cat, and he offered his companion reluctantly. He continued to work but became miserable and decided to run away. When he reached Highgate Hill, he heard the bells of the city calling "Turn again, Whittington, Lord Mayor of London." He returned and dis-

covered the ship had traded on an island overrun with rats, which his cat had vanquished. Dick was rewarded with a princely sum in exchange for letting the king of the island keep his cat. [And in fact, a man named Dick Whittington did hold the office of Lord Mayor of London—four times.]

Fairy-Tale Cat

THE NORWEGIAN FOREST CAT is a centuries-old breed originating in Norway, where it is called *Norsk Skaukatt*, or *Scogkatt*. It is believed that the Forest Cat may be the cat mentioned in some old Norwegian fairy tales, including a Scandinavian version of *Puss in Boots* where the villain is a troll. The Forest Cat keeps the troll talking until dawn, knowing that trolls perish in sunlight. Norse mythology also refers to a cat so huge even the god Thor could not lift it. With their bushy, soft, silky fur and wooly undercoats—not to mention full, feathered brush tail—perhaps it's true the cat that bested Thor was indeed the Norwegian Forest Cat?

The cat may have trimmed down a little since then. Affectionately known as Wegie in the United States, the Forest Cat is similar in appearance to the Maine Coon, though the head is shorter and more triangular. The cat is medium in size with superb jumping and climbing capabilities.

Forest Cats are also known for their prowess. Legend has it that early farmers prized the Forest Cat as a hunter and in lean times would rely on the cat's hunting ability to feed their families. The cats would hunt small animals and then share their catch.

Did You Know...

In 1879, a mail service in Belgium "hired" 37 cats to carry bundles of letters to villages near the town of Liege. The experiment didn't last long. As mail went astray, the cats were deemed "unreliable."

HOW MANY LIVES DOES KITTY HAVE?

IN AMERICA, the lucky feline has nine. She also has nine in Russia, though the Russian saying is that the cat will "survive nine deaths." According to Arab and Turkish proverbs, kitty better watch her step. They only allot her seven lives.

Why Nine Lives?

Why not 12 or 13? Some theories say nine is a lucky or holy number because it is the "Trinity of Trinities." With a cat's uncanny ability to bounce back and land on its feet, escaping danger time after time, this lucky number was thought well suited for our furry four-footed friends.

A cat has nine lives. For three he plays, for three he strays, and for the last three he stays.

—ENGLISH PROVERB

Feline Folk Sayings:

🐾 "When the cat's away, the mice will play."

🐾 "Honest as the cat when the meat's out of reach."

🐾 "The cat is mighty dignified until the dog comes by."

SPOTLIGHT SAYING: "IT'S RAINING CATS AND DOGS."

The origins of this popular saying remain murky. Several sources cite the Greek word *catadupe*, meaning *waterfall*, but that doesn't answer the question of how canines entered the equation.

Some claim the phrase has its roots in mythology. Cats were once thought to have an influence over storms. Witches were rumored to morph into cats to ride the wind. And dogs were associated with Odin, the god of storms.

The preferred answer to the phrase's origin comes from Northern European myths that associated cats with rain and dogs with wind. Thus rain and wind combined in a heavy gale would prompt the phrase: "It's raining cats and dogs."

Cats on Record:

Longest cat name? English poet Robert Southey (1774–1843) named his cat The Most Noble the Archduke Rumpelstizchen, Marquis Macbum, Earle Tomemange, Baron Raticide, Waowler, and Skaratchi. However, when calling the cat, Southey settled for the shortened Rumpel.

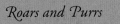"**A** black cat crossing your path signifies that the animal is going somewhere."

—GROUCHO MARX

IF SOMEONE CALLS YOU a "cat's paw," beware! "Cat's paw" refers to a person easily duped. The phrase originates with a not-so-flattering feline story. An ancient fable tells of a monkey who longed for chestnuts roasting in a nearby open fire. The devious monkey convinced a not-so-smart cat to reach in and grab the chestnuts for him. The monkey got his food, the cat nursed a hotfoot, and a phrase that's the equivalent of calling someone a "chump" was born.

Cat's Paw Nebula

WE MIGHT NOT BE READY to send cats into space (who would clean the litter box?) but that hasn't stopped them from leaving their mark there. The Cat's Paw Nebula, approximately 5,500 light years away, is shaped like a kitty's paw and glows red due to an abundance of hydrogen atoms. This nebula has birthed stars almost ten times as big as Earth's sun. Catnap at the Nebula, anyone?

CHINESE ZODIAC: YEAR OF THE TIGER

YOU'RE A TIGER if you were born in any of the following years: 1914, 1926, 1938, 1950, 1962, 1974, 1986, 1998.

People born in the Year of the Tiger are courageous and adventurous. They easily earn the respect of others but are prone to conflict with those in authority. Playful and powerful, they like to take risks and seek new adventures. Although sometimes short-tempered, people born under this sign are also known to be sensitive, generous, and contemplative. Tigers are compatible with horses, dragons, and dogs.

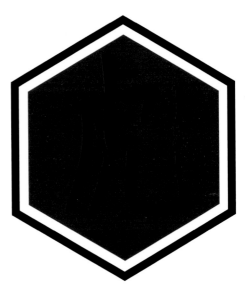

FAMOUS PEOPLE BORN IN THE YEAR OF THE TIGER:

Alec Guinness	Hilary Swank	Stevie Wonder
Karl Marx	Alanis Morissette	Leonardo DiCaprio
Marilyn Monroe	Dwight Eisenhower	Mel Brooks
Natalie Wood	Jay Leno	Tom Cruise

WESTERN ZODIAC: LEO

DOES YOUR BIRTHDAY fall between July 23 and August 22? Congratulations—you're a Leo!

Like the cats we love, Leos are ruled by the sun. People born under this sign exude warmth and caring. Known for being generous and warmhearted, Leos strive to be individuals in their own right. Their natural magnetism and gravity draw them to positions of leadership, though at times they can be bossy, dogmatic, and quick to judge. Overall, an expansive and creative spirit guides those fortunate enough to be born under this sign.

FAMOUS LEOS:

Andy Warhol	Lucille Ball	Henry Ford
Amelia Earhart	Napoleon Bonaparte	Jacqueline Kennedy Onassis
Mick Jagger	Magic Johnson	Robert De Niro
Dorothy Hamill	Robert Redford	Dustin Hoffman

Cat Festivals

Belgium Cat Festival: This popular festival is held every third year on the second Sunday in May in Ypres in the West Flanders province of Belgium. A cat-themed parade includes floats, costumes, and events based on feline mythology through the ages. The 40th celebration of the event took place in 2003.

Malaysia: In 1999, the Malaysian National Animal Welfare Foundation organized a ten-day cat festival to create public awareness of responsible pet owner- ship and pet therapy.

Thailand: In 2005, Phuket held its first annual Dog and Cat Festival. The festival included exhibition booths and dog and cat shows with participants from as far away as the Philippines.

Creole Cat Festival: Held in Dekattrois, Louisiana, the festival that honors the legend of the Creole Cat set an all-time attendance record in 1922 when an astounding 125,000 people attended in one day.

Marie Minou *by Chamain O'Mahony*

Then is it good *luck if I cross your path?*

Surviving "Cat"astrophes

IN NEW BRUNSWICK, teenage girls saved the lives of two kittens by performing an emergency C-section on a cat that had been hit and killed by a car. The teens recognized the animal and knew it was pregnant. When they checked and found that the cat's body was still warm, they decided to try and save the kittens, even though neither girl had any knowledge of cat anatomy. The girls were able to rescue two of the four kittens, bundling them in a sweater and taking them home. Later that same evening, a neighborhood cat that had recently delivered kits heard the mews of the newborns and adopted them.

"*H*ey Daddy-O, you're the cat's pajamas!" Meaning "great" or—in today's vernacular—"way cool," the saying originated in the 1920s when pajamas were still something of a novelty. The cat's pajamas kept good company along with "the bee's knees," "the duck's quack," "the tiger's stripes," and "the leopard's spots."

What's in a Phrase?

In the catbird seat: a high, commanding position; a position of power.

Cat burglar: a stealthy intruder able to enter premises undetected.

Catcall: shout, whistle, hiss, boo.

Catty: malicious, spiteful, mean, vicious, back-biting.

Fat cat: an important person; a wealthy person.

"Has the cat got your tongue?" Children were asked this during the mid-nineteenth century by parents trying to figure out if their child had been into mischief.

CATS ON RECORD

World's Smallest Cat: Mr. Peebles, named after a ventriloquist's dummy on an episode of *Seinfeld*, is a fully grown cat weighing a meager three pounds.

World's Longest Cat: Verismo's Leonetti Reserve Red (also known as Leo), a Maine Coon owned by a Chicago couple, measured 48 inches from nose to tail in March 2002.

Mr. Peebles (left)

World's Shortest Cat: Tinker Toy, a male Himalayan-Persian cat from the United States, measured 2.7 inches high and 7.5 inches long.

Longest Cat Whiskers: Another Maine Coon, this one named Mingo from Turku, Finland, set

Tinker Toy

the record for the longest single cat whisker on July 30, 2004. Mingo's whisker measured 6.8 inches.

Feline with Most Toes: Many cats are *polydactyl*, meaning they have extra toes, typically one or two on the front or back paws. However, an orange Tabby from Canada named Jake left all other polydactyl cats in the dust after his tootsies were counted—all 28 of them!

Longest Time Spent in a Tree: A female feline named Mincho may win the award for weirdest cat. Mincho climbed a tree in Argentina and didn't come down until she died six years later. She did not, however, allow the height to interfere with her social life. Mincho had three litters of kittens while up in the tree.

Cuty boy

Smartest Cat: Cuty boy, a Persian living in Bur Dubai, is no ordinary cat. In fact, some believe he may be the smartest cat in the world. According to his owners, Cuty boy can count to 20 (he "counts" by touching his nose to his owner's face), understands eight different languages, and can identify colors. Independent experts have confirmed that Cuty boy is indeed one talented feline.

Black Cat Crossing

- People in Britain and Japan believe a black cat crossing their path is a harbinger of *good* fortune.

- Scottish folks think a black kitten on the porch indicates happiness to come.

- Even better, according to Latvian farmers, is to find a black cat in your silo. This means Rungis, the god of harvests, has smiled upon you.

- Germans have to pay attention to direction to know whether they've been blessed or cursed. A black cat crossing their path from left to right is cause for celebration. Right to left, they might want to go in search of a four-leaf clover.

- Worse than a black cat crossing your path is *you* crossing *its* path. It is said that luck of the worst sort is sure to follow.

- *Crossing* the path of a black cat may be bad, but petting is always a good thing. Stroking a black cat is said to bring anyone health and prosperity.

- The Chinese believe black cats foretell times of famine and poverty.

🐾 According to Italians, if a black cat curls up on the bed of a sick person, death will soon follow.

🐾 Don't be anxious to rid your house of black felines. Chasing away a black cat is thought to seal the deal on bringing bad luck your way.

PLACES TO VISIT: THE CAT HOUSE

THE CAT HOUSE is a small store tucked away in Savannah, Georgia. Here you'll find all things cat—toys and collars, treats, note cards, throws, pillows, jewelry, handkerchiefs, T-shirts, and books.

You'll also find Hillary and Pocket, the cats who live and work at The Cat House. Black and white and weighing 16 pounds, Hillary is the dominant cat. According to store owner Janet Waters: "She's receptive to petting, especially from men and boys." She's also good with kids and practically allows toddlers to lay on top of her.

Pocket, a brown cat weighing 14 pounds, is the shyer of the two. He prefers to be petted only when on the counter by the register—his "safe zone."

Both cats consider The Cat House their personal inventory of toys and space. "I just pay rent," observes Waters.

Customers love coming in and seeing the cats, though sometimes they're startled by them.

"We have so much cat inventory, and people can be looking at it all when suddenly this cat moves in front of them," says Waters. "Their reaction is usually 'Oh! It's alive!'"

Nighty Night

RUSSIAN FOLK WISDOM says to throw a new cat into bed when you bring it home. If the cat settles down, it will stay with the new owner.

Gesundheit

AN OLD ITALIAN superstition says that a cat sneezing is good luck for anyone who hears it.

Did You Know...

🐾 In Britain, Persian cats are known as Longhairs.

🐾 The cat has been the most popular pet in Britain since the early 1990s.

🐾 Winston Churchill, a well-known cat lover, took his black cat Nelson with him when he became prime minister of Great Britain in 1940. A chair was held for Nelson next to Churchill in the Cabinet.

Winston Churchill

🐾 In medieval English pubs, "cat and kittens" was a common name for a pewter wine or beer jug with matching goblets.

🐾 British folklore holds that a young maid who loves cats or rocks a cat on her knee will never know marriage.

🐾 According to British tradition, the cats that are the best mousers are always given as gifts, never purchased.

POLITICAL TROUBLES

HUMPHREY, a large black-and-white cat, had ruled the British prime minister's official residence at 10 Downing Street for years. However, when Prime Minister Blair and his wife, Cherie—who was rumored to be less than fond of Humphrey—moved in, a statement was released saying Humphrey had retired and left the residence. Uneasy Brits feared the worst.

Amid a growing media frenzy, it was eventually revealed that Humphrey had been placed in a home in the suburbs where by all accounts he appeared most happy without the bustle and conundrum of city living.

Cherie Blair and Humphrey

Although Mrs. Blair hastened to assure the nation of her affection for cats, the story didn't truly die down until a group of journalists were actually taken to Humphrey's new residence to see that the feline was plump and content.

CHARTREUX (pronounced shar-true) is a native cat of France and the first recognized breed in Europe. Named for Le Grand Chartreux, a monastery in the French Alps outside Paris, the cats were first bred by Carthusian monks. The shape of this breed's head and ears blends gently into the soft lines of the body to resemble a monk's hood and robe. The Chartreux have been referred to as holy cats because the monks believed the cats kept the monastery holy by keeping vermin out.

The breed is known for its extremely dense blue-gray fur. On the sedentary side, the Chartreux enjoys bursts of activity and has been known to defend an owner in the presence of danger. Almost wiped out during the second World War due to lack of breeding, the Chartreux made a comeback by the late 1970s.

A tradition among Chartreux breeders is to assign letters of the alphabet to each year and name their cats accordingly; they start over when they run out of letters.

CATS ON RECORD

Oldest Cat to Give Birth: In 1987, a feline named Kitty gave birth at the ripe old age of 30.

Oldest Cat: Claims abound of cats having lived well beyond their prime years. However, the oldest *documented* cat is Creme Puff, who lives in Austin, Texas. She was born on August 3, 1967, and turned 38 in 2005.

Largest Collection of Cat Memorabilia: Florence Groff of France began collecting cat memorabilia after buying her first cat, Ulysses, in 1979. Since then, Florence has amassed 11,717 cat-related items including more than 2,000 cat figurines, 86 decorative plates, 140 metallic boxes, 9 lamps, 36 stuffed toys, 41 painted eggs, and close to 3,000 postcards.

Most Mice Caught: Towser, a tortoise-shell domestic cat kept as a pet in a Scottish distillery, owns the record for best mouser. Between April 21, 1963, and March 20, 1987, Towser caught an astounding 28,899 mice! The distillery erected a statue on the grounds to honor Towser and his devotion to duty.

Irish Proverbs

"Who would believe such pleasure from a wee ball o' fur?"

"A cat's eyes are windows enabling us to see into another world."

"Beware of people who dislike cats."

When something amuses a person in Ireland they say it's funny enough "to make a cat laugh."

A COMMON BELIEF held almost the world over is that every black cat has at least a single white hair. If you can tame kitty enough to pull the hair out (not to mention searching for it) without getting scratched, a happy marriage will be yours.

Likewise, many cultures believe in the healing power of the black cat. For example, passing the tail or even just a single hair from a black cat over an afflicted eye is noted to have cured everything from a sty to blindness.

Applause Please

DID YOU KNOW black cats are welcomed in the theater? That's because of numerous reported "black cat experiences": Actors have reported seeing a black cat before taking the stage and then delivering show-stopping performances. The black cat as good luck belief is so ingrained, many actors no longer leave it to chance and will show up with their own black cat to bring backstage with them.

CATERING TO THE CAT

THE MEOW MIX CAFÉ, a first of its kind restaurant for cats and their own-ers, opened on Manhattan's Fifth Avenue in New York on August 17, 2004. The establishment offered fine dining for felines with a choice of six cat foods. Instead of the "No Shirt, No Shoes, No Service" sign, management softened the dress code in favor of two new rules: no dogs and no catnip! For reasons unknown, the restaurant closed after only five days.

The Pampered Pussycat in historic Merchantville, New Jersey, has no such restric-tions. In fact, they recom-mend a Kitty Catbernet (treats in a plastic bottle) to complement the house specialty: Catnip Pizza.

Meow Mix Café

If you're in New Hope, Pennsylvania, don't miss the chance to check out Meow, Meow! Cat Lover's Emporium. The emporium has been serving cat-loving clients since 1988.

ash, or get licked.

Big Cat Facts

Who or what are the "big cats"? They are the cats of legend—felines whose roars may send a shiver down our spine. They are the lions, tigers, leopards, and jaguars.

Where Do Big Cats Roam?

🐾 Cheetah, Lion—Africa

🐾 Jaguar—Central and South America

🐾 Puma—North and South America

🐾 Leopard, Tiger—Asia

Big Cats by Weight (Average Weight of Males)

Tiger	350–640 pounds
Lion	370–500 pounds
Jaguar	220–350 pounds
Cougar	77–220 pounds
Leopard	110–200 pounds
Snow Leopard	60–120 pounds
Cheetah	75–119 pounds

- All big cats are spotted, at least for part of their lives—even the tiger, whose stripes may be considered "elongated spots."

- The puma is also known as a cougar, mountain lion, panther, catamount, or painted cat.

- The record numbers of people killed by single cats are as follows: 84 by a lion, 400 by a leopard, and 436 by a tiger.

- The cheetah is the fastest land mammal, with a top speed of 70 miles per hour.

- Only the lion, tiger, jaguar, and leopard can roar.

The Terminator Terminates Big-Cat Declawing

He's back, and this time he's helping cats. Governor Arnold Schwarzenegger signed AB 1857 into law on September 29, 2004, making California the first state to pass anti-declawing legislation in the United Sates. The law went into effect on January 1, 2005. It does not apply to domestic cats.

𝐀*fter dark all cats are leopards.*

—N<small>ATIVE</small> A<small>MERICAN</small> P<small>ROVERB</small>

THE FIRST CAT SHOW in America took place on March 6, 1881, at a museum on Broadway in New York City. However, this was merely a follow-up to the first modern cat show held at the Crystal Palace in south London in 1871. There, cat lover, writer, and artist Harrison Weir not only staged a successful show at London's leading public venue, attracting thousands, he also went on to write the definitive work *Our Cats*, which for a time would become the bible for cat show organizers.

Weir was named President of the first National Cat Club, founded in London in 1887, but resigned in disgust over members being more interested in collecting ribbons than in promoting the welfare of the feline.

The Cat Fanciers Association

*T*HE OLDEST American cat organization, CFA was founded in 1906. The first licensed CFA cat shows were held that same year in Buffalo and Detroit. Membership is restricted to breeders and exhibitors belonging to local cat clubs with a CFA affiliation. The association has grown since its humble beginnings— approximately 400 shows will be held worldwide this season.

COLIN POWELL MEETS COLIN POWELL

I**T'S HARD TO TELL** who has more medals—former Secretary of State Colin Powell or his namesake, CFA's 2003–2004 Cat of the Year, Caricature's Colin Powell. After being judged 290 times and beating out 22,700 cats in competition, the copper-eyed Bombay from Brookfield, Connecticut, finally got to meet the man for whom he was named. Colin the cat was presented to General Powell, former Chairman of the Joint Chiefs of Staff (the highest military position in the Department of Defense) in mid-August 2004.

The prize-winning cat was born on the first anniversary of the September 11 attacks. A somewhat rare breed, Bombays don't typically beat the more well-established breeds such as Persians and Siamese at the contest.

Colin Powell (the person) was given the honor of naming one of Colin the cat's male offspring. Holding with the owner's tradition of naming their cats after prominent African-Americans, the former Secretary of State named the cat Ralph Bunche, after the first African-American to receive a Nobel Peace Prize.

Colin Powell and his namesake

I am the cat of cats. I am
The everlasting cat!
Cunning, and old, and sleek as jam,
The everlasting cat!
I hunt the vermin in the night—
The everlasting cat!
For I see best without the light—
The everlasting cat!

—Anonymous, "The Cat of Cats"

CHAPTER FOUR

Do You Live Here Too?

"You don't own a cat.
The best you can do is be partners."
—SIR HARRY SWANSON

"**H**appy is
the home
with at least
one cat."

—Italian Proverb

Cats Overtake Dogs

S**TEP ASIDE** F**IDO**! It is the feline, not the pooch, that reigns supreme as the most popular pet in America. There are an estimated 90 million domestic cats in the United States compared to 73 million dogs. This translates to at least one cat in every three homes.

Playing Favorites

"**I**t's easy to understand why the cat has eclipsed the dog as modern America's favorite pet. People like pets to possess the same qualities they do. Cats are irresponsible and recognize no authority, yet are completely dependent on others for their material needs. Cats cannot be made to do anything useful. Cats are mean for the fun of it."

—P. J. O'ROURKE

"You can't look at a sleeping cat and be tense."

—JANE PAULEY

A window ledge is a wonderful thing.

CAT FACTS:

Did you know cats can get sunburned, even if they're not outdoors? Ultraviolet radiation travels through windows and can damage the delicate nose and ear tips of our feline friends. White cats are especially vulnerable. If your cat spends a great deal of time in the sun (is there a cat that doesn't?) consider applying small amounts of sunblock to the susceptible areas of skin, such as the bridge of the nose and the ear tips. You can also apply a line of sunblock along any part in the fur along the head or back. Add a pair of shades and a boogie board and your cat will be ready for summer fun.

Why do cats seek out such unusual places to sleep? The first kitty criterion is that the snoozing spot be free of drafts. Second, cats prefer to be hidden (the better to see you first, my dear!) and finally, cats like high places from which to survey their kingdoms.

The NAMING OF CATS is a difficult matter,
It isn't just one of your holiday games;
You may think at first I'm as mad as a hatter
When I tell you, a cat must have THREE DIFFERENT NAMES.
First of all, there's the name that the family use daily,
Such as Peter, Augustus, Alonzo or James,
Such as Victor or Jonathan, George or Bill Bailey—
All of them sensible everyday names.
There are fancier names if you think they sound sweeter,
Some for the gentlemen, some for the dames:
Such as Plato, Admetus, Electra, Demeter—
But all of them sensible everyday names.
But I tell you, a cat needs a name that's particular,
A name that's peculiar, and more dignified,
Else how can he keep up his tail perpendicular,
Or spread out his whiskers, or cherish his pride?
Of names of this kind, I can give you a quorum,
Such as Munkustrap, Quaxo, or Coricopat,

Such as Bombalurina, or else Jellylorum—
Names that never belong to more than one cat.
But above and beyond there's still one name left over,
And that is the name that you never will guess;
The name that no human research can discover—
But THE CAT HIMSELF KNOWS, and will never confess.
When you notice a cat in profound meditation,
The reason, I tell you, is always the same:
His mind is engaged in a rapt contemplation
Of the thought, of the thought, of the thought of his name:
His ineffable effable
Effanineffable
Deep and inscrutable singular Name.

—T. S. Eliot, "The Naming of Cats"

"**I** just found out why cats drink out of the toilet. My mother told me it's because the water is a lot colder in there, and I'm like, 'How did my mother know that?!'"

—Wendy Liebman

AMERICAN SHORTHAIR

WHEN THE MAYFLOWER reached the shores of the New World, the ancestor of the American Shorthair stepped onto Plymouth Rock with the rest of the pilgrims. American Shorthairs started out as mousers, keeping farms and homes free from vermin. Since then, they have retained their keen hunting abilities and are athletic cats, built for survival. They are much more playful and active as kittens than as mature cats and are slow to develop to their full adult size. Affectionate, head-butting cats that love to be petted, American Shorthairs tend to rule their families with an "iron paw." They thrive in the company of other cats but remain suspicious of strangers.

DID YOU KNOW...

The first registered American Shorthair came from a pedigreed bloodline introduced from England in 1900. Called a Domestic Shorthair until 1965, the breed began to gain devotees and was the first short-haired cat listed by the newly formed Cat Fanciers Association in 1906.

Top 20 Cat Names in the United States

1. Tigger
2. Tiger
3. Max
4. Smokey
5. Sam
6. Kitty
7. Sassy
8. Shadow
9. Simba
10. Patch
11. Lucky
12. Misty
13. Sammy
14. Princess
15. Oreo
16. Samantha
17. Charlie
18. Boots
19. Oliver
20. Lucy

"They say the test of literary power is whether a man can write an inscription. I say, 'Can he name a kitten?'"

—SAMUEL BUTLER

Lucy

I'M GOING TO CLOSE my eyes,
and when I open them I hope
there's a squeaky toy in front of me.
For your sake.

Cheap Tricks

🐾 Tie a string to just about anything, and pull the object along the floor. Watch kitty stalk and pounce!

🐾 Drop an ice cube on the kitchen floor for an impromptu game of ice hockey.

🐾 Goldfish (safely contained!) are good for hours of meditative gazing.

🐾 Turn on a faucet so kitty can have some water playtime.

🐾 Hide a feather or cotton mouse underneath pillows, a T-shirt, or a loose pile of newspapers. Cats love hidden prey.

🐾 Place some kibble in a treat ball, and make kitty work for his dinner. He won't even realize he's exercising.

🐾 Table-tennis balls in the bathtub. Does it get any better?

DID YOU KNOW ...

Grooming behavior after play is a sign your cat is tuckered out and wants to rest.

"*When I play with my cat, who knows if I am not a pastime to her more than she to me?*"
—MICHEL DE MONTAIGNE

"*Once it has given its love,*
what absolute confidence,
what fidelity of affection!
It will make itself the companion
of your hours of work, of loneliness, or of sadness.
It will lie the whole evening on your knee,
purring and happy in your society,
and leaving the company of creatures
of its own society to be with you."

—Théophile Gautier

Cats make excellent paperweights.

"The phrase 'domestic cat' is an oxymoron."

—George F. Will

What's in a Purr?

EXPERTS CAN'T AGREE on how cats manage the purr. And so far, cats aren't telling! What we do know is vibrating purrs are a means of feline communication. It's how a kitten sends the "all's well" signal to its mother. It's also how our cats indicate "Yes, that's the spot!" during their nightly rubdown. Whatever the cause, a purr is surely a soothing mantra to both feline and human souls.

"A cat can be trusted to purr when she is pleased, which is more than can be said for other human beings."

—WILLIAM RALPH INGE

"Even if you have just destroyed a Ming Vase, purr. Usually all will be forgiven."

—LENNY RUBENSTEIN

Where's that Cat?

*B*EST PLACES TO LOOK: behind the books in the bookshelf, any cupboard with a gap too small for any cat to squeeze through, the top of anything sheer, under anything too low for a cat to squash under and inside the piano.

—ROSEANNE AMBROSE-BROWN

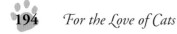

"*A kitten is a rosebud in the garden of the animal kingdom.*"

—ROBERT SOUTHEY

RAGDOLL

"**T**HE BIGGER THEY ARE, the harder the fall" may apply to cat lovers who fall head over heels in love with Ragdolls, the largest of all the domestic cat breeds. Males weigh anywhere from 15–20 pounds and measure 18 inches in height.

Descended from a white Persian in California in the 1960s, Ragdolls have thick, soft fur that increases in length from the head to the tail. Their coat comes in either solid point, mitted (white mittens on the legs), or bicolor patterns. They are very large, long cats with gentle, trusting natures. Indeed, Ragdolls have an aversion to fighting or even protesting when made uncomfortable. They have earned the nickname "three feet of love" because of their accommodating nature. They like everything and everyone, enjoy both company and solitude, and are definite nesters.

As for the name, Ragdolls are prone to collapsing in a limp heap when picked up, just like holding a rag doll. This, along with their retiring nature, has sparked the rumor that Ragdolls have a high tolerance for pain. However, Ragdoll breeders say that the Ragdoll's pain threshold is no different from that of any other breed.

$\mathcal{A}$CCORDING TO THE American Animal Hospital Association of Lakewood, Colorado, close to 70 percent of pet owners say they break household rules with their pet when their spouse or significant other is not present. Women are more likely to break the rules than men.

Top Ten Most Popular Pedigreed Breeds for 2004

(CFA registration statistics)

1. Persian
2. Maine Coon
3. Exotic
4. Siamese
5. Abyssinian
6. Ragdoll
7. Birman
8. Oriental
9. American Shorthair
10. Tonkinese

WHAT'S IN A BREED?

- Persian: Fluffy cats known for their quiet, affectionate demeanor. Said to be the most gentle of all cat breeds.

- Siamese & Oriental: The most vocal of all breeds. Outwardly demonstrative and affectionate, often territorial, highly inquisitive.

- Burmese: Inquisitive but also known for their sensitive and trusting nature.

- British, European, and American Shorthairs: Loving, demonstrative cats.

Mistaken Identity

AN INTENSE THREE-WEEK search for a black panther reported loose in the French city of Marseille was called off when the "panther" turned out to be a very large black house cat. The cat was approximately 24 inches long and weighed 22 pounds. No doubt the city of Marseille slept better that night.

After a long day of lying on the sofa,
I like to unwind by rolling over for a stretch and a nap.

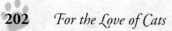

SINGAPURA

FOUR UNUSUAL CATS were sent from Singapore to Texas in 1971; one cat died, but the other three reproduced. In 1974, their grandchildren went back to Singapore, and when they returned to the United States in 1975, they were registered as a new breed.

Weighing in at 4–6 pounds, the Singapura is the smallest of all breeds. Considered rare, the cats are somewhat compact yet lithe with rounded heads, short muzzles, and large almond-shape eyes. Their short, brown, ticked coat resembles an Abyssinian's but is silkier. Singapuras only come in sable-ticked tabby.

OTHER RARE BREEDS

- American Bobtail
- American Curl
- Burmilla
- California Spangled
- Malayan
- Munchkin
- Ragdoll
- Safari
- Selkirk Rex
- Siberian
- Snowshoe
- Sphynx
- Tiffany

Native to Singapore, this breed earned the name "Drain Cat" as the cats sought shelter and a place to nap in the sewers of the bustling city. Since mice and rats dwelled in these areas, the cats hunted them and thrived.

Singapuras are quiet, gentle, and alert. They are loyal and prefer to be with one person. Like Ragdolls, they are nesters. And although small in stature, Singapuras have a purr that belongs to cats twice their size.

The Lazy Cat

CATS SLEEP AN AVERAGE of 16 hours per day.
That means a six-year-old cat will only have
spent about two years of his life awake!

NEDJEM (meaning "sweet" or "pleasant") is the first documented cat name. It dates from the reign of Thutmose III (1479 B.C.–1425 B.C.) in Egypt.

To teach kitty her name, avoid using abbreviations and instead use the same name each time you address her. Reward kitty with a treat when she looks at you when you say her name.

Snowball or Fluffy? Cats respond best to names ending in the "ee" sound.

"Cats always seem so very wise,
when staring with their half-closed eyes.
Can they be thinking, 'I'll be nice,
and maybe she will feed me twice?'"

—Bette Midler

Notes from a Cat: How to Keep Your Owner Happy

1. Resist the urge to show them your backside every time they enter a room.

2. Remind yourself, the suitcase is *not* for peeing in.

3. Hop in their laps while they're watching TV and start purring. Humans need to be reminded that real life is more interesting than sitcoms.

4. Do not jump from behind closed doors to attack the dog (or at least restrict yourself to no more than twice a day).

5. Twine yourself between your owner's legs no matter what they're doing. Bonus points apply if they are carrying something heavy.

6. Allow them to think it's their idea that all the comfy chairs in the house are reserved for you.

7. Rub your head on all available surfaces to mark what's yours. Owners will appreciate this clear delineation of who owns what.

8. Every once in a while, allow them to pet your belly. It feeds their souls.

ALTHOUGH BEST KNOWN for his principles of gravity, Sir Isaac Newton (1642–1727) is also credited with inventing the first cat flap. As the story goes, Newton was in his attic conducting light experiments but was disturbed when his cat nudged open the door and let in the light. To accommodate his beloved cat's comings and goings, Newton cut a flap in the door. His cat was then able to enter and exit the room without disturbing his work.

The story doesn't end there. It seems even the most brilliant of minds can be blindsided by love for their cats. Once his cat had kittens, Newton cut a second, smaller hole alongside the first for the kittens to use. Apparently it didn't occur to Newton that all the cats could use the same hole.

Cat Proverbs

"**B**ooks and cats and
fair-haired little girls
make the best furnishing
for a room."
—FRENCH PROVERB

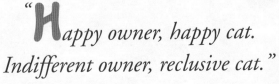

"**H**appy owner, happy cat.
Indifferent owner, reclusive cat."
—CHINESE PROVERB

Home Away from Home

LAS VEGAS IS CATERING to more than players. America Cat and Dog Hotel is an 11,000-square-foot, state-of-the-art pet hotel consisting of private suites, kitty villas, and a 5,000-square-foot play area. There are 14 private luxury suites, which come complete with an attendant who plays with, brushes, and walks the "suite babies" (dogs and cats) while Mommy and Daddy hit the casinos and shows. For cats, the hotel offers a Mediterranean stucco village consisting of 13 luxury three-story cat villas each with stained glass windows, color TV, private kitchen, bathroom, and study.

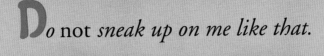

Do not *sneak up on me like that.*

MYTH VS. FACT

DOMESTIC CATS DON'T CRAVE the wild outdoors and hand-to-mouth existence of their ancestors. In fact, a cat that has been raised indoors usually has no desire to go out. This translates into longer lives for our cats. The life expectancy of cats has nearly doubled since 1930—up from 8 years to 16 years. The explanation given for the increase in life expectancy is that more cat lovers are keeping their cats indoors and safe from cars, dogs, and other outside hazards. For feral cats, the average life span is a fleeting two years.

Feral Cats

A 1997 STUDY ESTIMATES the homeless cat population in America to be between 26 million in the winter and 40 million in the summer. Feral cats range from the truly untamed (born and raised in the wild) to domestic cats that have been abandoned. Feral cat colonies form in urban, suburban, and rural settings. A movement is taking place for "capture, spay/neuter, and release" to at least stem the flow of new cats.

DID YOU KNOW...

A single pair of cats and their kittens can produce as many as 420,000 kittens in just seven years.

Anywhere from 7 percent to 25 percent of American households are feeding stray cats.

Cats put the spread in bedspread.

"When dogs leap onto your bed, it's because they adore being with you. When cats leap onto your bed, it's because they adore your bed."

—Alisha Everett

"Cats are rather delicate creatures and they are subject to a good many ailments, but I never heard of one who suffered from insomnia."

—Joseph Wood Krutch

Say Cheese!

How to Take a Picture of Your Cat

🐾 Let kitty pose herself.

🐾 Use props to catch kitty in an action pose.

🐾 "I'm ready for my close-up." Fill 70 percent of the shot with kitty's face.

🐾 Get on your cat's level. Kneel, squat, or lie on the rug. Photos are more interesting if you're at the same level as kitty.

🐾 Move fast and take lots of shots. Most won't turn out but the more you take the better you'll get and the more gems you'll find. Worry less about getting the "purr-fect" shot and instead just have fun.

🐾 Leave your camera out for impromptu shots.

MYTH VS. FACT

What causes cat allergies?

CONTRARY TO POPULAR BELIEF, it's not dander, cat fur, or saliva. Instead, it's a fatty protein called *sebum*, which is secreted by a cat's sebaceous glands (found under the skin and primarily located around the base of the tail). These glands help keep a cat's coat healthy and shiny.

Sebum flakes off in particles so small they can adhere to just about anything. Clothes, carpet, and furniture are prime targets. Even a thorough cleaning may not do the trick—the allergen can remain in the home for months or even years after kitty has vacated the premises.

CAT FACTS:

- It's estimated that 2–15 percent of people in the world are allergic to cats—and a third of them keep cats in the home anyway.

- People who are allergic to one cat may not be allergic to another.

- Male cats shed the allergen in much greater amounts than females. A neutered male, on the other hand, sheds significantly less.

- Many cats in shelters were placed there by allergic pet owners.

Mission:
Window
shade pull
string.

Decision:
Accepted.

Cool Cat Quotes

"**A**s every cat owner knows, nobody owns a cat."
—Ellen Perry Berkeley

"**I** have studied many philosophers and many cats. The wisdom of cats is infinitely superior."
—Hippolyte Taine

"**T**here is nothing in the animal world, to my mind, more delightful than grown cats at play. They are so swift and light and graceful, so subtle and designing, and yet so richly comic."
—Monica Edwards

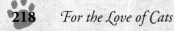

"**Y**ou see the beauty of the world
Through eyes of unalloyed content,
And in my study chair upcurled,
Move me to pensive wonderment.
I wish I knew your trick of thought,
The perfect balance of your ways;
They seem an inspiration, caught
From other laws in older days."

—Anonymous

CHAPTER FIVE

Cat'itude!

"The cat has too much spirit to have no heart."
—ERNEST MENAUL

Tattle Tails

A telltale clue to a cat's mood is the position of his tail. A mere flick of the tail can relay a message worth a thousand words.

- 🐾 A vertical tail indicates a friendly welcome.

- 🐾 An upright tail bent forward displays dominance.

- 🐾 A wagging tail can signal ambivalence, anger, or annoyance.

- 🐾 When the tail curves down and up, kitty is calm and content.

DID YOU KNOW...

Ten percent of a cat's bones are in its tail. The tail helps the cat to maintain balance when jumping or running.

"*A cat has absolute emotional honesty:
human beings, for one reason or another,
may hide their feelings, but a cat does not.*"
—ERNEST HEMINGWAY

Why Don't Cats Wash Before They Eat?

*A*s LEGEND GOES, the cat once caught a mouse and was about to eat the tasty little morsel when the mouse chided the cat for her bad manners. "What?" cried the mouse, "You're going to eat me without first washing your face and hands?"

The mortified cat immediately dropped the mouse and began washing, and the clever little mouse quickly ran away.

Ever since, cats have not washed before dinner.

—AESOP'S FABLES

"Cats seem to go on the principle that it never does any harm to ask for what you want."

—Joseph Wood Krutch

MAINE COON

THE MOST ROMANTIC—if highly improbable—tale of the Maine Coon's beginnings involves the French Queen Marie Antoinette of "Let them eat cake" fame. The story holds that at the start of the French Revolution, Ms. Antoinette made plans with a Captain Samuel Clough to smuggle her to Wiscasset, Maine. The queen sent six of her Persian and Angora cats to the ship in advance but was herself detained. Captain Clough set sail for the United States, where Marie's cats were said to have bred with domestic American cats to produce the all-American Maine Coon.

If that story isn't to your liking, an old folktale holds the breed was the result of a cross between a raccoon and a semi-feral domesticated cat. Although the exact origin of Maine Coons remains cloaked, this natural longhaired breed probably shares some of the same ancestors as Norwegian Forest Cats.

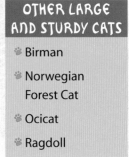

OTHER LARGE AND STURDY CATS

- Birman
- Norwegian Forest Cat
- Ocicat
- Ragdoll

Maine Coons are fun-loving and friendly. Known as "gentle giants," they are loyal to their owners and will patrol their homes to guard against intruders. They are especially good with dogs and children. Champion hunters from their early days as farm cats, Maine Coons have a sturdy body with a long, full tail that tapers to a tip. Their thick longhaired coat comes in all colors and patterns and was developed as a result of the severe New England climate. Indeed, they seem almost impervious to the elements.

Sometimes referred to as "Coon Cats," they have a quiet voice and talk in sweet chirps and twitters; they sometimes sound so much like birds that people wonder where the "songs" are coming from.

A Maine Coon was chosen Best Cat at the first major cat show ever held in the United States.

Hold the Milk

CONTRARY TO POPULAR BELIEF, you should not give a kitten cow's milk. It has too much sugar. However, if you have any sheep's milk hidden away in the fridge, kitty would be most grateful.

How many dogs does it take to screw in a lightbulb? All of 'em. One to turn it and the rest to run around in circles and bark at it!

SOMETHING SMELLS FISHY

A FELINE'S SENSE OF SMELL is 14 times stronger than a human's. Compared to our cats, we are blind, deaf, and scent-dumb. Cats use smell not only to reject the dinner you've set out for them (although that does seem to be their favorite use) but also for identification, communication, and navigation.

Cats can even smell with their mouth! "Flehming" involves two extra scent organs found between the hard palate of the mouth and the septum of the cat's nose. The grimacing, lip-curling behavior transfers scent particles with the tongue to tiny ducts behind the upper front teeth where they connect to the special scent organs. Flehming actually falls somewhere between smelling and tasting.

DID YOU KNOW...

* Newborn kittens smell their mother and literally follow their noses to find her. By the age of three weeks, kittens will have the same highly developed sense of smell as an adult cat.

* People tend to carry the most interesting smells on their purses, briefcases, and hands. By smelling those items thoroughly, your cat gets a good idea of where you've been, what you've done, and even (sacrilege!) if you've petted another cat.

* Cats dislike the smell of chlorine and are adept at detecting even minute amounts of it in tap water. This is why kitty might turn her nose up at a fresh bowl of water and instead lap from a less-than-clean looking pond or puddle.

"Some pussies' coats are yellow;
Some amber streaked with dark,
No member of the feline race but has a special mark.
This one has feet with hoarfrost tipped;
That one has tail that curls;
Another's inky hide is striped;
Another's decked with pearls."

—ANONYMOUS

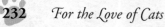

"The most domestic cat, which has lain on a rug all her days, appears quite at home in the woods, and, by her sly and stealthy behavior, proves herself more native there than the regular inhabitants."

—Henry David Thoreau

The Eyes Have It

*T*HE COLOR OF A kitten's eyes change as it grows older. All kittens are born with blue eyes, and it takes about three months before they change to their final adult color. Kittens' eyes first open between day 6 and day 12 of life. It takes another two or three days before they can see. By 10 weeks of age, their sense of sight is fully developed.

*"*I*t is in their eyes that their magic resides."*

—ARTHUR SYMONS

Did You Know...

- Cats can't see in total darkness, but they need only one-sixth as much light as we do.

- Cats can see blue, green, and yellow hues (but prefer mousy-gray shades!).

- Relative to body size, cats have the largest eyes of any mammal.

- Feline eyes were designed for the hunt; they give a cat nearly 285 degrees of dimensional sight.

- The reflectors in the middle of the road that bounce your headlights back to you at night are called "cat's eyes" and were designed to mimic the way a real cat's eyes reflect light.

- Cats' eyes may be large, medium, or small, but all cats have round eyes.

- The color of a cat's eyes are determined genetically and can range from copper to blue.

- Balinese have the closest set eyes of any breed; their eyes are only one eye width apart.

"**C**uriosity killed the cat,
Satisfaction brought it back!"

—ENGLISH PROVERB

Dog Shmog.

BALINESE

ALTHOUGH THEY ARE 100 percent American, Balinese were named after the graceful movement of dancers from the Isle of Bali and the parent Siamese cat. The Balinese is a longhaired version of the Siamese cat, a natural spontaneous mutation. Aside from hair length, the cats are nearly identical. Like the Siamese, these cats love their families and have been known to risk their lives— even fighting off armed burglars—to protect them.

Balinese cats are very intelligent. They can open doors and drawers with ease, but once they are trained, they remember—even if they don't always obey—the words "no" and "come here."

These cats are talkers and alternate between being extremely active and surprisingly sedentary. Balinese cats are also demanding but are so lovable and affectionate that their owners will forgive them for nearly anything.

Balinese are soft and lovely to look at since the longer hair forms an aureole of softness around their limber bodies. According to legend, the aureole was referred to as a veil, and the cat's body was said to move like that of a Balinese dancer surrounded by her swirling, silken veils. Today it's easy to see that every move these cats make is dancelike—they are truly grace in motion.

Even cats can have bad hair days.

How to Give a Cat a Pill

1. Sit on sofa. Pick up cat and cradle it in the crook of your elbow as though you were going to give a bottle to a baby. Talk softly to it.

2. With right hand, stroke cat's throat until it opens its mouth (be patient). Drop pill into mouth. Let go of cat, noticing the direction it runs.

3. Pick the pill up off the floor and go get the cat. Sit on floor in kitchen, wrap arm around cat as before, drop pill in mouth. Let go of cat, noticing the direction it runs.

4. Scoot across floor to pick up pill, and go find the cat. Bring it back into the kitchen. Hold cat as before, but hold down its front paws with forearm. Drop pill into mouth.

5. Pry claws from back legs out of your arm. Go get the cat, pick up half-dissolved pill from floor and drop it into garbage can.

6. Get new pill from bottle. Go into bathroom, and get a fluffy towel. Stay in the bathroom with the cat, and close the door.

7. Sit on bathroom floor, wrap towel around kitty, leaving only his head exposed. Cradle kitty in the crook of your arm, and pick up pill off of counter.

8. Retrieve cat from top of shower door (you didn't know that cats can jump five feet straight up in the air, did you?), and wrap towel around it a little tighter, making sure its paws can't come out this time. With fingers at either side of its jaw, pry it open and pop pill into mouth. Quickly close mouth (his, not yours).

9. Sit on floor with cat in your lap, stroking it under the chin and talking gently to it for at least a half hour, while the pill dissolves.

10. Unwrap towel, open bathroom door. Wash scratches in warm soapy water, comb your hair, and go find something to occupy your time for seven hours, then repeat.

This Is All Mine

ＥVER NOTICE KITTY walking around the house, rubbing his cheek against wall corners and the couch? He's leaving behind a scent mark saying, in effect, "This is mine." Scent glands are found in kitty's cheeks, temple, chin, and even his tail and paws. So when you're the recipient of a face rub or a tail curling around your legs, that's kitty's affectionate way of claiming you as his own.

"There is no shame in not knowing ... the shame lies in not finding out."

—Russian Proverb

Lap It Up

Cats drink by curling their tongue into a spoon-shape scoop. They lap the liquid, flicking each scoop to the back of their mouth and swallowing after every four or five laps. The rough center surface of their tongue acts like a sponge to retain water.

Cats remind us not to keep things bottled up.

ABYSSINIAN: THE BUNNY CAT

ONE OF THE OLDEST recognized breeds is the Abyssinian. Some believe the Abyssinian cat was the Bast cat worshipped in ancient Egypt. This could be because Abyssinians resemble the Egyptian Kephyr cats in color and body type. The ancient Egyptians used Kephyr cats to eliminate disease-carrying pests.

In 1868, a solider returning from war brought a cat called Zula from Abyssinia to Great Britain. This cat had a unique ticked coat and was bred with other cats with similar markings. From these matings, the Abyssinian breed was produced.

As kittens, Abyssinians are frequently referred to as chipmunks. Active and frisky, these cats retain their love for play as they mature. Of all the breeds, Abys are the most demonstrative of their love. They are one-person cats and will pick their favorite human out of a family, remaining alert, intelligent, and sensitive to their person's moods. Abys will tolerate other cats but are not group-oriented. While not known as cuddlers, they will march up your lap, put their paws on your chest, and demand to be petted while purring up a storm.

MYTH VERSUS FACT
Do cats always land on their feet?

MOST OF THE TIME, yes. The feline righting mechanism works in combination with balance organs in the middle ear and sight sense. When she falls, kitty first turns her head to an upright position, then with a series of twists and turns of her flexible spine, the rest of her body follows. But the righting mechanism doesn't prevent injuries. Cats falling short distances might not have time to turn and land properly.

"A kitten is so flexible that she is almost double; the hind parts are equivalent to another kitten with which the forepart plays. She does not discover that her tail belongs to her until you tread on it."

—Henry David Thoreau

"Cat's motto: No matter what you've done wrong, always try to make it look like the dog did it."

—Unknown

I "Knead" You

WHY DO CATS TREAD and knead with their paws when content? As kittens, tiny paws push rhythmically against mom's belly to stimulate the release of milk. Adult cats who knead are thought to be remembering back to their carefree kitten days. So take it as a compliment when kitty gives you a mini-paw massage ... she's saying she needs you!

THE FOX AND THE CAT

A Fox was boasting to a Cat of its clever devices for escaping its enemies. "I have a whole bag of tricks," he said, "which contains a hundred ways of escaping my enemies."

"I have only one," said the Cat; "but I can generally manage with that." Just at that moment they heard the cry of a pack of hounds coming toward them, and the Cat immediately scampered up a tree and hid herself in the boughs. "This is my plan," said the Cat. "What are you going to do?" The Fox thought first of one way, then of another, and while he was debating the hounds came nearer and nearer, and at last the Fox in his confusion was caught up by the hounds and was soon killed by the hunters. Miss Puss, who had been looking on, said:

"Better one safe way than a hundred on which you cannot reckon."

—Aesop's Fables

Nature breaks through the eyes of a cat.
—IRISH PROVERB

Scaredy Cats

- To calm a frightened cat, place your hands over its eyes or allow him to bury his head in your lap or armpit until he calms down.

- A frightened cat can sprint up to 31 miles per hour.

- Try gently stroking a cat's forehead to relieve stress or anxiety.

- Cats can leap up to six times their body length.

- In martial arts, the "cat stance" allows for quick blocking, attacking, and leaping out of the way of an attack. It is best known for the narrow distance between the front and rear legs.

You are getting sleepy.

Your eyelids are getting heavy.

You want to give me a big can of tuna.

"A cat is there when you call her— if she doesn't have something better to do."

—Bill Adler

LET'S "HEAR IT" FOR THE CAT

KITTY'S EARS SWIVEL like radar detectors as she takes note of what's going on around her. The cat's hearing is among the sharpest in the animal kingdom—they can recognize their owner's footsteps from hundreds of feet away! Cats don't even have to move their heads to know which direction a sound is coming from. Instead, they just maneuver their ears. People can detect lower tones than cats but felines far outhear us in the high ranges. For example, high-pitched mouse squeaks come in at 40,000 cycles per second. No problem for the feline, who can hear sounds up to the 65,000-cycle range (but problematic for the human, who can hear only up to the 23,000-cycle range). For the most accurate indication of a cat's mood, look at the position of his ears. Confident, curious cats turn their ears forward so they won't miss a thing.

Cat'itude! **259**

- Just like snowflakes or human fingerprints, no two cat nose prints are exactly the same.

- A breeding female is called a *queen*.

- A castrated male is a *gib*.

- A "head bonk" is what happens when an affectionate cat nudges you with the front part of its head.

- Cats have about 100 different vocalization sounds. In comparison, dogs have about 10.

- A group of cats is called a *clowder*.

- The giraffe, camel, and cat are the only animals that step with both left legs then both right legs when they walk (as opposed to alternating left and right).

- A cat uses its whiskers to "feel" its environment.

- A cat's heart beats twice as fast as a human heart: 110–140 beats per minute.

- Presenting an unprotected tummy indicates trust.

"**A** cat pours his body on the floor like water.
It is restful just to see him."

—William Lyon Phelps

Did You Know...

* Cat owners in the United States spend approximately *two billion* dollars on cat food each year.

* Twenty percent of cats don't care for catnip.

* Obesity is a growing concern among pet owners. The National Research Council of the National Academy of Sciences estimates obesity will occur in 25 percent of dogs and cats.

* Scientists have tried to make a "mouse flavored" cat food, but so far no luck. Cats have hated the taste.

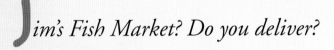

Jim's Fish Market? Do you deliver?

MYTH VERSUS FACT

"White cats make bad mothers."

THE REALITY IS that some white cats are born with congenital hearing loss that results in deafness. Such cats wouldn't be able to hear kittens cry, which may be how the myth started. Hearing loss affects about one in every five white cats; longhaired cats are more often affected than short-haired ones. Also, deafness is more common in blue-eyed white cats. Interestingly, some white cats with one blue eye are only deaf on that side.

CAT FACT:

Ever notice how one little noise can render a seemingly comatose cat instantly wide-awake? Cats jump back to full alertness faster than any other animal.

Did You Know...

🐾 Cats have no specific blood type and can donate across breeds.

🐾 Cats lack a true collarbone. That's how felines end up in odd places. Generally, cats can squeeze into any space they can fit their heads into.

🐾 Adult cats have 32 teeth.

🐾 Cats have right and left "hands" just like people. Forty percent are right-pawed, 20 percent are left-pawed, and a lucky 40 percent of cats are ambidextrous.

🐾 Human bites are more dangerous than cat bites because people have more bacteria in their mouths.

🐾 There are 245 bones in a cat's body compared to 206 in an adult human's.

🐾 Cats are digitigrades. That means they walk on their toes—a great skill for sneaking up on prey!

🐾 A 1997 survey indicated 33 percent of cat owners believed that their feline responded to their unspoken commands.

One should be
just as careful in
choosing one's
pleasures as in
avoiding
calamities.

—Chinese Proverb

KAY DRAPER HAD a problem. After exiting the cat box filled with ashes—common to the 1940s household—her kitty would leave ashy paw prints all over the house. What was an American housewife to do?

She mentioned her problem to her neighbor and friend, Edward Lowe, who suggested she try absorbent clay. Ms. Draper loved the clay and refused to use anything else for her cat.

Witnessing his neighbor's loyalty to the clay, Lowe decided to market it. He packed it in 5-pound bags, marked "Kitty Litter" on the side, and tried to sell it to pet stores for sixty-five cents. The first store owner turned him away. Sand and ashes were cheap, and he didn't think people would pay for Lowe's clay product.

DID YOU KNOW...

❧ Thomas Nelson, a biochemist, invented clumping litter in 1984.

❧ Traditional clay litters such as Lowe first produced still account for 40 percent of the cat litter market today.

❧ Clumping litter accounts for 60 percent of the cat litter sold in the United States.

He was wrong. Lowe convinced the pet store owner to give his clay kitty litter away as samples, and soon cat lovers were clamoring for it. Lowe went on to establish Edward Lowe Industries, Inc., and in 1964 created the Tidy Cat® brand of kitty litter. Edward Lowe Industries went on to become the largest producer of kitty litter in the United States. When Lowe sold his company in 1990, it was earning more than $210 million a year in kitty litter sales.

With the qualities of cleanliness, discretion, affection, patience, dignity, and courage that cats have, how many of us, I ask you, would be capable of being cats?"

—FERNAND MERY

I *won't roll in* that *again.*

"To *bathe a cat takes brute force, perseverance, courage of conviction—and a cat. The last ingredient is usually hardest to come by.*"

—Stephen Baker

Cat'itude! **269**

SCOTTISH FOLD

SCOTTISH FOLDS ARE instantly recognizable by their unique folded ears. The ears crease forward and down, giving the Fold an endearing, surprised, kittenlike expression.

Discovered by a shepherd in Scotland at a farm where he worked, Susie was the first cat with folded-down ears. When she had a litter of kittens, two of them had this same type of ear. The new breed was named the Scottish Fold. Loving, quiet cats, they get along well with other pets but crave human companionship. With tiny voices not often used, they are nonetheless heavy-boned, well muscled, and sturdy in appearance. They love to hunt and are particularly resistant to diseases.

Interestingly, Scottish Fold kittens are born with straight ears. At three to four weeks the ears will either stay straight or fold over. Straight-ear Scottish Folds may still be used for breeding.

An old tale explains the origin of these unusual ears. It was said that the howling of the winds across the moors and the wailing of the bagpipes caused these cats to fold down their ears, shutting out the cold and the wailing music.

"**H**e that can
have patience
can have what
he will."

—Benjamin Franklin

I trust my dinner is ready and waiting for me in its usual spot.

MYTH VERSUS FACT

Maternity

AN ENDURING MYTH argues that having kittens is good for a cat, but there is no medical evidence to support this argument.

DID YOU KNOW ...

Female felines are "superfecund," which means that it's possible that each kitten in a litter has a different father.

*If you ever need a sign of God's benevolence,
remember it was he who gave us cats.*

CHAPTER SIX

Best Friends

"*It is a matter to gain the affection of a cat. He is a philosophical animal, tenacious of his own habits, fond of order and neatness, and disinclined to extravagant sentiment. He will be your friend, if he finds you worthy of friendship, but not your slave.*"

—THEOPHILE GAUTIER

*W*HO SAYS cats and dogs are sworn enemies? A four-year-old calico cat named Sparky proved otherwise when she came to the rescue of her friend and housemate, a poodle named Lacy Jane, in Dora, Alabama. Lacy Jane had just gone outside when her owner heard barks and growls and rushed out to find Lacy Jane being attacked by an aggressive pit bull. Sparky, who was on the porch ten feet away, took a running leap and landed on the pit bull's head, spitting, scratching, and clawing for all she was worth. Lacy Jane was saved when the pit bull finally managed to shake Sparky off and darted away.

"The cat could very well be man's best friend
but would never stoop to admitting it."

—Doug Larson

IGUANA-CAT THERAPY

L IZ PALIKA AND HER HUSBAND, Paul, do reptile rescue in California, taking in unwanted pet reptiles and finding them new homes. Conan, a green iguana, had been a pet-store mascot, well loved and very spoiled, when some teenage burglars broke into the store and stole him. After weeks of abuse, Conan was found by the police. When the Palikas took him in, he was traumatized and scared and wanted nothing to do with the pair of humans. However, Xena, the Palikas' three-year-old tabby (herself a rescue), decided to take Conan on as her special project. Within weeks, the two diverse species, prey and predator, had established a rapport and would bask in the afternoon sun together. Conan observed as Xena allowed herself to be handled and petted by the Palikas. Slowly, the iguana began to allow his new owners to handle him. Within months, thanks to Xena's example, Conan was again the calm, gentle iguana he used to be. Conan was adopted by a new home where he now lives contentedly with several feline friends.

Cats and Women

"I have found my love of cats most helpful in understanding women."

—John Simon

"The dog for the man, the cat for the woman."

—English Proverb

"Women and cats will do as they please, and men and dogs should relax and get used to the idea."

—Robert A. Heinlein

"I've never understood why women love cats. Cats are independent, they don't listen, they don't come in when you call, they like to stay out all night, and when they're home they like to be left alone and sleep. In other words, every quality that women hate in a man, they love in a cat."

—Jay Leno

YIN AND YANG, black-and-white feline brothers, consider themselves staff members at the San Francisco SPCA Hearing Dog Program. The program has trained more than 750 dogs to be aides for hearing-impaired individuals, and Yin and Yang take a personal interest in every dog that enters the program.

The cats joined the staff when Training Coordinator Glenn Martyn noticed the dogs became overexcited when encountering the downstairs office cats. Martyn asked permission to find a cat to live at the program's training facility, then discovered Yin and Yang on a trip to Montana.

Easygoing and playful, Yang was the more immediately sociable of the two, approaching dogs and even initiating playful wrestling matches with smaller breeds.

Yin was more laid-back, choosing to ignore the dogs until they came close and then batting at them when his personal space was invaded. For a while, Yin's favorite game was to lie underneath the telephone table and wait for a dog to come over so he could swat at it. "Not so great when we're trying to train a dog to respond to the telephone," explains Martyn.

Observing how the staff trained the dogs to use their mouth and paws to open cabinets, Yin and Yang learned to do the same. This proved problematic when the duo figured out the apartment window had a similar latch. "We had to redo the window to keep them from getting out to 'play' with the pigeons they so admire," says Martyn.

The Chinese yin-yang symbol denotes balance and harmony in life.
For up, there is down. For black, there is white. And for dogs at
The San Francisco Hearing Dog Program, there will always be cats.

Hear our prayer, Lord, for all animals,
May they be well-fed and well-trained and happy;
Protect them from hunger and fear and suffering;
And, we pray, protect specially, dear Lord,
The little cat who is the companion of our home,
Keep her safe as she goes abroad,
And bring her back to comfort us.

—RUSSIAN PRAYER

Cat Stats

- In one study, when asked, "Who listens to you best?" 45 percent of respondents chose their pet, while only 30 percent chose their spouse or significant other.

- The majority of Americans (94 percent) think their pet has humanlike personality traits.

- In case of natural disasters such as flood or earth-quake, 55 percent of Americans have an emergency preparedness plan that includes their pet.

- Studies have shown that stroking a cat can lower your blood pressure. Pet owners agreed—59 percent say pets are good for their health and that of their family.

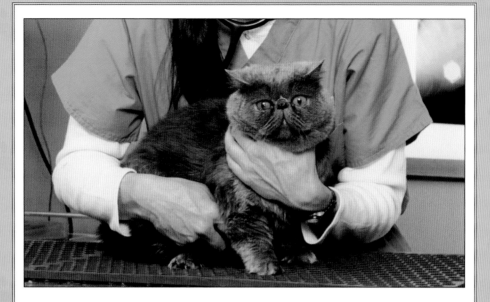

- A surprising 58 percent of Americans see their pet's veterinarian more often than they see their own physician.

- If away from home during the day, 82 percent of Americans think of their pet more than once.

- If marooned on an island and able to choose only one companion, 50 percent of Americans would pick a dog or cat over a human.

- Willing to risk your life for your pet? You're not alone: 93 percent of respondents would do the same.

Ears. Scratch. Now.

"**C**ats do not declare their love much; they enact it,
by their myriad invocations of our pleasure."

—Vicki Hearne

"**C**at people are different to the extent that they generally are not conformists. How could they be with a cat running their lives?"

—Louis J. Camuti, D.V.M.

NOT ON MY WATCH...

A BLACK-AND-WHITE CAT named Duchess saved a sleeping family in Texas by repeatedly throwing herself against their closed bedroom door. Getting up to see what Duchess needed, the family discovered their mobile home was on fire. The smoke alarm never sounded. They were able to get everyone to safety, thanks to the alarm sent by Duchess.

Gizmo, a Burmese cat living in Colorado, was given a hero award for awakening his owner from a heavy medication-induced sleep. The cat jumped on his owner, meowing and pawing. The reason for Gizmo's attentions? The electric blanket the owner was sleeping under had caught fire.

For Me?

DID YOU KNOW...

- Five percent of cat owners have thrown their cat a birthday party.
- Sixty-three percent of cat owners purchase gifts for their feline friends on birthdays, holidays, and just for the fun of it.
- The cost of the average cat gift? $17.
- Popular gifts include catnip toys, cotton mice, jingle balls, a new collar, a water fountain, oat grass, and anything Garfield.

Did I not mention that this was mine?

*W*HO KNOWS WHERE the heart will lead? A leopard from a village in India decided to start paying nightly visits to a cow. According to wildlife warden Rohit Vyas, "It was unbelievable. They approached each other at very close proximity and the fearless cow would lick the leopard on its head and neck."

The leopard showed no interest in harming or befriending other animals in the village, and the villagers actually welcomed the nightly visits from the leopard, which kept other crop-damaging animals at bay.

The forest department decided against trapping the leopard, much to the delight of both cow and cat.

SOMETHING TO CROW ABOUT...

CASSIE, a black-and-white kitten, was abandoned in the Massachusetts backyard of Ann and Wally Collito. As the Collitos set about caring for the kitten, they noticed someone else taking an interest—a wild crow they nicknamed Moses. "Moe the Crow" would take the food the Collitos set out for Cassie and place it in her mouth. "She trusted no one but the bird," says Ann. If Cassie wandered too near the street, Moe did everything possible to turn her back. The

two also played together, roughhousing, tumbling, and exploring the yard. Eventually, Cassie came to trust the Collitos as well. But no one was as special to her as her adopted dad Moe. "They make a beautiful team," states Ann. "I think they'll always be the best of friends."

Horrible conflict? Or three unlikely friends playing a game?

Top Ten Ways Humans Resemble Cats

1. We're convinced the world revolves around us.

2. We'll never turn down a back massage.

3. We sometimes hide when people come to the door.

4. We like to stare at ourselves in the mirror.

5. We can nap anytime, anywhere, regardless of appropriateness or noise levels.

6. All our toys bore us after the first five minutes.

7. We believe in the value of snuggling.

8. We're not so sure about the intelligence level of dogs.

9. Sometimes we run around for no apparent reason.

10. We'd rather torture people by making them guess what we want versus just telling them outright.

*I*t isn't the size of the human.
It's the size of the love in the human.

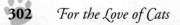

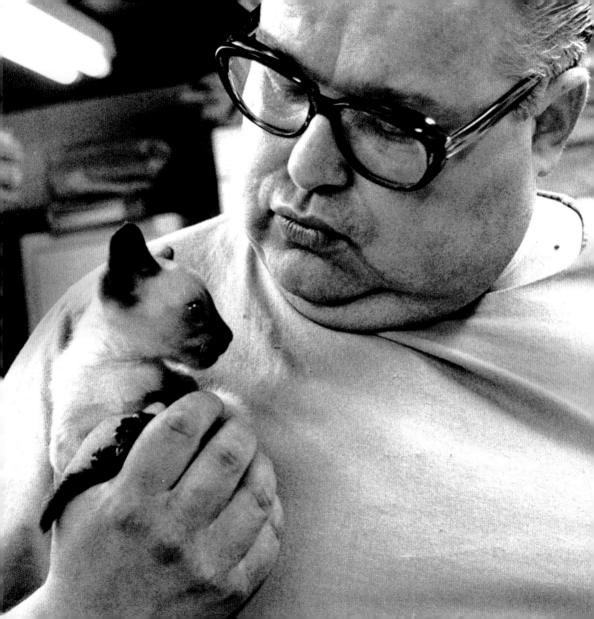

AN AMAZING JOURNEY

SUGAR WAS A CREAM Persian who became famous when her family moved from California to Oklahoma—and she followed.

The family started the journey with Sugar in the car, but the Persian was so obviously ill and terrified that the family reluctantly turned around and left Sugar in the care of trusted neighbors. Fighting back tears, the family waved good-bye to Sugar as they set out once again for Oklahoma.

Fifteen days later the neighbors wrote to say Sugar had disappeared, and despite their frantic attempts to locate her, she was nowhere to be found.

Fast-forward 14 months. Sugar's original owner was doing the family wash when a bedraggled Persian jumped through an open window and landed on her shoulder. Upon examination, the owner joyously recognized the cat as Sugar. Sugar had been injured years earlier in a road accident and had an unmistakable scar on her hind leg.

In order to be reunited with her family, Sugar had walked more than 1,500 miles, crossing not only the Great American Desert but the Rocky Mountains as well. Prior to this journey, Sugar had never strayed farther than the next-door neighbor's backyard.

Better than a Glass Slipper

In 1955 in Keston, England, a cat named Ginny came limping home to her owner. The owner removed what appeared to be a piece of glass from Ginny's left front paw. On further inspection, the "glass" turned out to be two diamonds—each worth about $600!

Time spent with cats is never wasted.

—COLETTE

 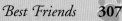

Did You Know...

- A cat's yawn means he trusts you enough to relax.

- Cats touch each other as a means of bonding and establishing their hierarchy. A nose-to-nose greeting between friendly cats is a sign of affection.

- Camilla, a cat in Portugal, walked 125 miles to find her way home to her owners.

- Dr. Samuel Johnson, poet and essayist, used to go out and purchase oysters for his beloved cat Hodge. He could have sent servants but feared they might dislike the cat if asked to perform the task.

"**I**n order to keep a true perspective of one's importance, everyone should have a dog that will worship him and a cat that will ignore him."

—DEREKE BRUCE

"Cats are possessed of a shy, retiring
nature, cajoling, haughty, and capricious,
difficult to fathom. They reveal themselves
only to certain favored individuals, and are
repelled by the faintest suggestion of insult
or even by the most trifling deception."

—PIERRE LOTI

"**C**ats don't bark and act brave when they see something small in fur or feathers, they kill it. Dogs tend to bravado. They're braggarts. In the great evolutionary drama the dog is Sergeant Bilko, the cat is Rambo."

—JAMES GORMAN

Things I Have Learned from My Cats:

🐾 Make the world your playground.

🐾 Whenever you miss the sandbox, cover it up.
   Dragging a sock over it helps.

🐾 If you can't get your way, lie across the keyboard till you do.

🐾 When you are hungry,
   meow loudly so they feed
   you just to shut you up.

🐾 Always find a good
   patch of sun to nap in.

🐾 Nap often.

🐾 When in trouble, just
   purr and look cute.

🐾 Life is hard, and then
   you nap.

🐾 Curiosity never killed anything except maybe a few hours.

🐾 When in doubt, cop an attitude.

🐾 Variety is the spice of life. One day, ignore people; the next day annoy them, and play with them when they're busy.

🐾 Climb your way to the top, that's why the curtains are there.

🐾 Make your mark in the world, or at least spray in each corner.

🐾 Always give generously; a bird or rodent left on the bed tells them, "I care."

—INTERNET: AUTHOR UNKNOWN

The real voyage of discovery consists not in seeking new landscapes but in having new eyes.

—Marcel Proust

Index